FOODIE

TOP 100

RESTAURANTS

Worldwide

EAT WELL
WHILE YOU TRAVEL

— DAN

FOODIE

TOP 100

RESTAURANTS

Worldwide

SELECTED BY
THE WORLD'S TOP FOOD CRITICS
AND GLAM MEDIA'S FOODIE EDITORS

BY GLAM MEDIA

CHRONICLE BOOKS
SAN FRANCISCO

Editor:
Samir Arora

Food Critics:
Patricia Wells
Gael Greene
Masuhiro Yamamoto
Ruth Reichl
Jonathan Gold
Bruno Verjus
Alexander Lobrano
Charles Campion
Vir Sanghvi
Aun Koh
Susumu Ohta
Kundo Koyama
Yuki Yamamura

Managing Executive Editor:
Erika Lenkert

Library of Congress Cataloging-in-Publication Data available.

ISBN 9781452127910

Manufactured in the United States of America

Design by Bonni Evensen

Facebook is a trademark of Facebook, Inc. Craigslist is a trademark of
Craigslist, Inc.

10 9 8 7 6 5 4 3 2 1

Chronicle Books LLC
680 Second Street
San Francisco, CA 94107
www.chroniclebooks.com/custom

CONTENTS

Welcome

Dear Food Lover,

It is with great pleasure that I introduce the inaugural edition of Glam Media's *Foodie Top 100 Restaurants* guide.

Why create an all-new guide now, especially a print book, when there are other, well-established print guides and myriad user reviews on the Internet?

As a lifelong foodie, I was fortunate that much of my childhood was spent inside the kitchens in our multigenerational family restaurants. My early memories are of watching food being created, served, and eaten with great passion and love. Little did I know that I would leave my family food business to work at a young company called Apple Computer and end up running a media company focused on style and food.

The *Foodie Top 100* guide started with a simple idea—that it would be amazing to bring together the knowledge of the world's top critics and our editors to create a list of the world's best restaurants whose main criteria is the quality of the food. For me, it would provide the ultimate answer to the question: How can I discover a great sushi restaurant, whether in Tokyo or New York, based on the recommendations of experts who actually know about sushi? With this guide, we have provided that answer and then some.

Three critical elements make this guide different from other "best of" restaurant lists.

First is our belief that the knowledge and experience of the world's top food critics and our editors is essential to picking the world's top restaurants. We selected the critics who contributed to this book because they are the very best in the business and have been advising food lovers for decades. We combined their nominations with our own before curating the list into the world's top 100 restaurants. We also created our first regional top 100 restaurants lists for France; Japan; the United States; and Europe, the United Kingdom, and Asia Pacific and included them as a bonus.

Culinary expertise was not enough, however, to justify each contribution. To create an up-to-date, fair list of the truly best places, we only allowed critics and editors, including myself, to nominate restaurants that they had visited recently, and no one could nominate a restaurant that he or she is professionally tied to.

The second critical element is our nomination criteria: "food first." To be included, all the restaurants had to lead with exceptional food and outstanding menus. Their service, décor, and drinks programs were considered only as complements to what was on the plate and their style of cooking. Our goal was to find the best world-class food experiences, regardless of whether it fit the classic "fine dining" or "award-winning wine list" profiles. As a result, ancillary bells and whistles—such as molecular orchestrations, a massive wine list, incredible architecture, and dining room theatrics—did not increase a restaurant's chances of being part of this list. The food must be spectacular; everything else is secondary. We believe this less-narrow approach to defining the "best" restaurants allows for a better, more diverse, and truly outstanding list of the places where serious foodies should make a point of dining.

The third differentiator is accessibility. We wanted to make our lists available through a variety of channels. So even though Glam Media is an online digital company reaching more than 470 million users each month, we invested in a printed book in addition to our website Foodie.com and mobile applications for the iPhone, iPad, and Android devices.

I want to take a moment to extend my deepest gratitude to chefs worldwide, especially those featured within these pages. This book celebrates the passion that drives you and your teams and the gifts you give us as diners.

Bon appétit!

SAMIR ARORA
PUBLISHER AND EDITOR
FOODIE TOP 100 RESTAURANTS WORLDWIDE

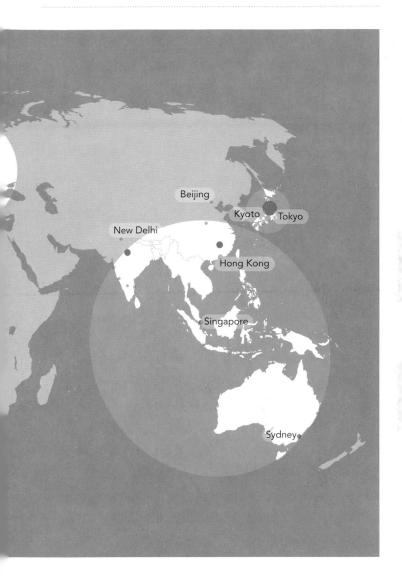

Foodie Top 100 Restaurants Worldwide

Introduction

Welcome to the *Foodie Top 100 Restaurants Worldwide* guide. Within the following pages you will discover the finest restaurants across the globe as determined by a carefully selected group of the world's top food critics and our own Foodie editors.

In addition to showcasing each of the 100 top restaurants with vibrant photographs and critical facts, we provide more nuanced information that will help enhance your dining experiences, including insider tips from our critics and editors—such as what to order, where to request to be seated, and when to go. You'll also find symbols, when applicable, beneath each restaurant's name. Designed with the serious food lover in mind, these icons provide important insight into each establishment's offerings, strengths, and specialties. See the following page to learn about our symbols and their meanings.

At the back of the book you will discover bonus Top 100 lists for France; Japan; the United States; and Europe, the United Kingdom, and Asia Pacific.

We hope the guidance provided here leads you to many new exceptional dining experiences.

Additional information about our top 100 restaurants and the regional top 100 lists can be found at www.Foodie.com.

FOOD CRITICS AND NOMINATING EDITORS

Samir Arora (Editor)
Patricia Wells (France)
Gael Greene (USA)
Masuhiro Yamamoto (Japan)
Ruth Reichl (USA)
Jonathan Gold (USA)
Bruno Verjus (France)
Alexander Lobrano (France)

Charles Campion (U.K.)
Vir Sanghvi (India)
Aun Koh (Asia)
Susumu Ohta (Japan)
Kundo Koyama (Japan)
Yuki Yamamura
(Japan: Foodie Editor)

Foodie Top 100 Symbols

Look for these symbols beneath each restaurant's name for more insight into the establishment.

 Fixed-Price Menu Only
Guests must order a multicourse meal; à la carte options are not offered.

 Traditional
The restaurant is emblematic of traditional food, décor, and customs.

 Modern Cuisine
The kitchen is known for molecular gastronomy, other cutting-edge cooking techniques, or both.

 Organic Focus
The establishment is extremely focused on using organic ingredients whenever possible.

 Local Ingredients Focus
The menu primarily features ingredients sourced from the immediate surrounding area.

 Ecological Practices
The restaurant practices environmental sustainability through ingredients selection, recycling, and carbon-emission reduction.

 Exceptional Drinks Program
The establishment features an especially fantastic wine, beer, or sake list, superb cocktails, or all four.

 Scenic
The destination boasts truly exceptional views.

 Outdoor
Weather permitting, the establishment features alfresco dining.

 Romantic
The ambience is especially romantic.

 Private Dining
The restaurant has dedicated private areas for special meals or events.

 Chef's Table
There is exclusive designated seating in the restaurant's kitchen where diners can sit, eat, and watch the chefs in action.

Special Events
The establishment offers ongoing seasonal dinners, guest winemakers, or other special events.

Cash Only
No credit cards are accepted here. Meals must be paid for with cash.

FRANCE

TURBOT OVER SWISS CHARD WITH BABY SHELLFISH

ALAIN DUCASSE AU PLAZA ATHÉNÉE

[FRENCH] Any notion of French haute cuisine as dull or passé is quickly dispelled by a meal at this illustrious Alain Ducasse outpost, where Chef Christophe Saintagne interprets fine dining in a fresh, even earthy way. His streamlined, abbreviated menu makes exquisite ingredients the main event without a touch of preciousness. The first course of langoustines with crème fraîche and caviar, a signature dish presented in perfect bite-size portions, is brilliant in its simplicity. Main courses, perhaps including turbot resting on a fragrant bed of Swiss chard accompanied by a delicate fish broth and an array of baby shellfish (pictured at left), also allow the ingredients to elegantly shine. Complementing the meal, the service by absolutely charming Maître d'Hôtel Denis Courtiade— one of the best in Paris—is tailored to the style and desires of each table, while Sommelier Laurent Roucayrol warmly helps navigate the impressive wine list. In an opulent dining room glowing with a 10,000-crystal "decomposed chandelier," Alain Ducasse continues to shine as one of the brightest lights of Paris fine dining.

CRITICS' TIPS

Try for a table overlooking the interior courtyard. These are the best seats in a wonderful house.

If you have never visited a grand, efficient restaurant kitchen, be sure to ask for a quick look before the meal.

Order the lobster. If it's not on the menu, ask for it and give the kitchen carte blanche in preparing it.

HÔTEL PLAZA ATHÉNÉE
25 AVENUE MONTAIGNE
75008 PARIS, FRANCE
+33 (0)1 53 67 65 00
WWW.ALAIN-DUCASSE.COM/EN/RESTAURANT/
ALAIN-DUCASSE-AU-PLAZA-ATHÉNÉE

LANGOUSTINE TAILS, SPINACH, AND SESAME WAFERS OVER
LIGHT CURRY SAUCE

L'AMBROISIE

[FRENCH] French haute cuisine doesn't get much more altitudinous than here, where the most expensive and revered meal in France is a direct reflection of its perfectionist chefs Bernard and Mathieu Pacaud. A regal establishment set in Paris's chic place des Vosges, L'Ambroisie prides itself on the purity and quality of its ingredients and eschews the cutting edge for the classic. The elements here are simple—excellent products tended to with perfected techniques and unmatched attention to detail that let the ingredients' inherent flavors dazzle. Two shining examples are the *bel humeur* ("beautiful mood") *feuilleté de truffe fraîche*, a black truffle– and foie gras– filled puff pastry set on a bed of truffle purée, and the *feuillantine de langoustines aux grains de sesame*, expertly prepared langoustines served amid two crisp sesame wafers floating on a bed of curry sauce (pictured at left). The décor, like the food, is unpretentiously luxurious; simple tabletops adorned with modest flower arrangements, the finest cutlery, and tapestries contribute to the private-club atmosphere. Elegant maître d' Pascal Vettoux adds the finishing polish, running the restaurant with quiet old-world perfection.

CRITICS' TIPS

This is one of France's most romantic settings, so seize the opportunity to walk around the place des Vosges before or after your meal.

If it is on the menu, order Pacaud's escalopines de bar, émincé d'artichauts, nages reduit au caviar. *It's sea bass, artichoke, and caviar heaven.*

Don't miss Chef Pacaud's densely flavored yet feather-light chocolate tart.

9 PLACE DES VOSGES
75004 PARIS, FRANCE
+33 (0)1 42 78 51 45
WWW.AMBROISIE-PARIS.COM

NAPA CABBAGE STUFFED WITH CABBAGE, DILL, AND BLACK RADISH

L'ARPÈGE

[MODERN FRENCH] Chef Alain Passard named this Paris gem for one of his passions—music—but it's his love of vegetables that makes L'Arpège sing. While the menu is not strictly vegetarian, you will never have more exciting vegetable dishes than you will here, because Passard grows many of his own ingredients in three nearby gardens and often serves them the same day they're harvested. A restaurant signature, the "hot cold" egg features warm egg yolk served in the shell and bathed in sherry vinegar, maple syrup, salt, spices, and chilled cream. The blend of sweet and tart, hot and cold, offers an intriguing start to the meal. A sweet-onion gratin, the color of marigolds, has the haunting taste of candied lemon threaded throughout like a musical note, promises one of our critics. Vegetable "sushi"—an exquisite, nori-wrapped rice dish draped with a gorgeous slice of vegetable—makes fish seem irrelevant, though Passard's seafood offerings are as delicate as his produce. Regardless, be prepared for creative experiments on the plate, as nothing here is done in the "usual" way. An extensive wine list, exceptional cheese plate, and desserts, such as a sublime *tarte au pommes*, complete a surprising dining experience.

CRITICS' TIPS

Consider visiting during spring or summer, when vegetables are at their peak.

Don't miss the fresh vegetable juices, which shine on their own and in cocktails.

If available, try the langoustine two ways, which shows the depth of Passard's French culinary expertise and talent.

84 RUE DE VARENNE
75007 PARIS, FRANCE
+33 (0)1 47 05 09 06
WWW.ALAIN-PASSARD.COM

ROASTED VENISON WITH CHILE PEPPER AND JUJUBE

L'ASTRANCE

[CONTEMPORARY FRENCH] While it may look as though little has changed since Chef Pascal Barbot and partner Christophe Rohat opened this venerable restaurant in 2000, their wildly creative cuisine continues to outdo itself. With no written menu, each meal is carefully choreographed by the talented, cerebral Chef Barbot according to what's freshest and in season. Often tinged with notes of citrus, spices, and herbs, with added depth of flavor from a variety of Asian ingredients, his surprising globally influenced French fare is as stunning on the plate as it is on the palate. Among some of Barbot's standouts: foie gras marinated in *verjus* served with a galette of white button mushrooms; baby ravioli filled with *cédrat* (citron); and chile pepper sorbet paired with lemongrass and ginger. Even a simple brioche transcends when adorned with salty rosemary-lemon butter. Barbot's profound knowledge of classical French technique informs his cooking, yet he never hesitates to be puckishly irreverent. Fitting of this serious yet whimsical dining experience, Maître d'Hôtel Rohat leavens the codes of French formal dining with warmth and a sense of humor.

CRITICS' TIPS

Consider reserving a table for lunch, when reservations are easier to come by.

For an especially romantic interlude, request the single table in the mezzanine.

FOIE GRAS AND APPLE BRAISED UNDER NOBLE WOOD ASH

L'ATELIER DE JOËL ROBUCHON
SAINT-GERMAIN

[FRENCH] After Joël Robuchon, rightly considered one of the most revered chefs in the world, closed his flagship restaurant in Paris, his L'Atelier quickly became "the next best thing." Eschewing fine-dining convention, Robuchon takes reservations for only the first seating; the rest of the night is first-come, first-served. The restaurant seems to have taken design cues from classic sushi restaurants, with tables facing a dramatically lit black-and-red counter behind which chefs in black uniforms with red piping can be seen whipping up culinary revelations under the watchful eye of Head Chef Axel Manes and, on some days, Chef Robuchon himself. Signature dishes include what one of our critics proclaims the world's best mashed potatoes. Also heralded is satiny foie gras in port jelly under a layer of Parmesan cream, caviar in a jelly on a rich cauliflower cream, and sea urchin cream with a wasabi emulsion. Despite the lack of formality, the cuisine is anything but lackadaisical. Rich yet modern, it's French decadence defined— full flavored, focused, and indicative of why Chef Robuchon remains one of the world's top culinary inspirations.

CRITICS' TIPS

If you don't have a reservation, expect a wait—and expect that when you are seated it will be on a stool, which is the only type of seat in the house.

Don't think you need to have a full dinner here. You are welcome to come just for a snack.

Consider coming on "off" restaurant days: unlike many Parisian restaurants, this one is open Sunday and Monday.

5 RUE DE MONTALEMBERT
75007 PARIS, FRANCE
+33 (0)1 42 22 56 56
WWW.ATELIER-ROBUCHON.COM

GAMMA
kitchen from the Arclinea Collection

Arclinea
since 1925

ARCLINEA SAN FRANCISCO

91 3rd Street San Francisco

CA 94103 415 543 0771

www.arclineasanfrancisco.com

TOP 10 WINE DIRECTORS AND SOMMELIERS

Behind every great wine program is a great individual. The following 10 wine professionals deserve recognition for not only curating exciting lists but also providing a level of service that elevates the overall dining experience and sets the standard for wine service worldwide.

Michael Acheson
The Village Pub
Woodside, CA, USA

Patrick Borras
Pierre Gagnaire
Paris, France

Patrick Lair
Laurent
Paris, France

Gérard Margeon
Alain Ducasse Enterprise
Paris, France/Worldwide

Rajat Parr
Michael Mina and RN74
San Francisco, CA, USA

Marco Pelletier
Epicure
Paris, France

Aldo Sohm
Le Bernardin
New York, NY, USA

Seigo Takei
Keiko à Nob Hill
San Francisco, CA, USA

Rajeev Vaidya
Daniel
New York, NY, USA

Eiji Wakabayashi
Esquisse
Tokyo, Japan

WILD TURBOT WITH STEAMED ROOT VEGETABLES

CARRÉ DES FEUILLANTS

[MODERN FRENCH] Alain Dutournier may be Paris's most winning ambassador for France's southwest. Using many of his native region's finest ingredients, he updates the traditional cuisine to match the restaurant's sleek, modern setting. Just off the place Vendôme, in rooms with Venetian-glass chandeliers and sophisticated hues, Dutournier creates a varying menu that showcases both his love for the region as well as his talent. His reverence for each ingredient is apparent even in a simple bouillon, which enamors with its scent of chestnuts and white truffles. A tartine of paper-thin chestnut slices and warm toast slathered with white-truffle butter add to its delectability. An alabaster turbot fillet topped with caviar from France's Aquitaine may arrive on a bed of al dente black rice, a sophisticated play on black and white, smooth and crunchy. As one critic describes it, it's a brilliant chef treating noble ingredients with intelligence and creativity. Dutournier's exciting 3,500-bottle wine list pays homage to the greats of Bordeaux and well-priced treasures of the Southwest, but it also features international offerings and superb Armagnacs, all of which are easily navigated with the help of the knowledgeable staff.

CRITICS' TIPS

Try the whole fish on or off the menu—it's sure to be superb.

Order the outstanding cheese course, and don't miss the fougeru affiné, *a bloomy-rind cow's milk cheese from Champagne that has been sliced in half, filled with a blend of mascarpone and minced white truffles, then reconstructed.*

For exceptional value, come during lunch and order from one of the varied bargain menus.

14 RUE DE CASTIGLIONE
75001 PARIS, FRANCE
+33 (0)1 42 86 82 82
WWW.CARREDESFEUILLANTS.FR

ROTISSERIE-ROASTED POITOU SQUAB WITH BRAISED *RATTE* POTATOES, ONIONS, AND LARDONS

LE COQ RICO

[MODERN FRENCH] Alsatian Antoine Westermann's third restaurant, this rotisserie-meets-bistro is a single-ingredient concept squarely focused on gourmet interpretations of pedigree poultry. Within the modern space with white-on-white décor and an open kitchen and counter, the whole bird is celebrated, from farm fresh eggs that can be ordered any way you like to gizzards to guinea fowl. While the kitchen, presided over by Chef Thierry Lébé, is known for its whole rotisserie-roasted farm-raised chickens—such as Challans, Coucou de Rennes, Géline de Touraine, and the pièce de résistance, the whole roasted Bresse hen—other signature dishes merit consideration. The foie gras ravioli is one such example. Served in an intense, deep broth of poultry and celery root with *planchette de béatille*s—seared poultry hearts, tenderly cooked gizzards, and glazed wings—and little deep-fried balls of herbs, it's dazzling. According to one critic, the fries, which come solo or with any roast chicken alongside jus and a seasonal green salad, are about the best ever—"deep golden brown, crispy, can't-stop-eating-them delicious." For dessert, the classic *île flottante,* or meringue floating on crème anglaise, is flawless.

CRITICS' TIPS

If you're part of a larger group, reserve the communal table in the back room, which seats up to 16 guests.

Before ordering, consider that a whole roasted chicken serves two to four people, depending on appetite.

Follow the locals to one of the best deals in Paris: the plat du jour.

98 RUE LEPIC
75018 PARIS, FRANCE
+33 (0)1 42 59 82 89
WWW.LECOQRICO.COM

SMOKED GOAT CHEESE RAVIOLI WITH FOREST MUSHROOMS AND
TONKA BEAN FOAM

LA DAME DE PIC

[MODERN FRENCH] Located near the Louvre, Anne-Sophie Pic's sensational fourth restaurant—and first in Paris—La Dame de Pic, or the "queen of spades," shows her at the top of her game. The space, designed by Philippe Starck protégé Bruno Borrione, merges masculine and feminine with crystal lamps and mirrors, crisp white-linen table runners, and modern wooden tables punctuated by vases holding single long-stemmed blooms. Intending to surprise and delight, each selection of set menus features a striking and sensual concept, such as "Vanilla Amber" or "The Sea & Flowers." Throughout, ingredients are impeccable, preparations are complicated but not overdone, and the taste theme is one of softness and smoothness with a requisite touch of crunch. Visit and you may marvel at a regal, cloudlike presentation of warm Gillardeau oysters bathed in a frank and fragrant cream of cauliflower and jasmine or a vibrant pea soup (*le petit pois de montagne*) flavored with a touch of licorice and galanga, which tastes as though the peas were picked in the palace gardens only seconds before.

CRITICS' TIPS

Expect your dining experience to begin before you order. The three aromatic-themed meals offered each night are presented on paper menus infused with scent for your first sense-awakening "taste."

Flavored butters are not to be missed—one green anise, another thé matcha—both carefully, if not sparingly, spread on whole wheat or rye-miso bread.

Don't pass up the cheese course: three perfectly aged Picodon goat's milk cheeses from Pic's home region of Drôme.

20 RUE DU LOUVRE
75001 PARIS, FRANCE
+33 (0)1 42 60 40 40
WWW.LADAMEDEPIC.FR

PARMESAN-GRATINATED MACARONI STUFFED WITH BLACK TRUFFLE, ARTICHOKE, AND DUCK FOIE GRAS

EPICURE

[MODERN FRENCH] Set in the famed Bristol Hotel in the fashionable eighth arrondissement, Epicure is as luxurious as it gets. Recently relocated within the property to a new Pierre-Yves Rochon–designed space with an exquisitely manicured courtyard garden, it offers one the best examples of modern French food. Chef de Cuisine Eric Frechon, who hails from the Parisian kitchens of Taillevent, La Tour d'Argent, and Le Crillon, oversees inventive cuisine that's simultaneously modern and classic, taking all the traditional rhythms and making them look and taste anew through innovative molecular and contemporary techniques, while remaining profoundly true to his roots. Exemplary dishes include crab claws stacked and bound together with tangy green tomato gelée, sole stuffed with tiny wild mushrooms, and his signature dish, macaroni stuffed with artichokes, black truffle, duck foie gras, and Parmesan cheese (pictured at left). Artfully executed and presented, each dish exudes an intensity of flavors that inspires one critic to coo, "Mushrooms taste more like mushrooms, basil tastes more like basil, a tomato tastes more like a tomato." Complementing the meal is the expertise of Restaurant Manager Frédéric Kaiser and the talents of Marco Pelletier, one of the world's friendliest top sommeliers.

CRITICS' TIPS

Dress accordingly. Ties are not required, but jackets are.

Anticipate stargazing; it's a great place to watch for movers and shakers, including regular Nicolas Sarkozy.

Don't hesitate to reserve a table for one or for a weekend lunch; this is one Paris restaurant that graciously accommodates both.

LE BRISTOL PARIS
112 RUE DU FAUBOURG SAINT-HONORÉ
75008 PARIS, FRANCE
+33 (0)1 53 43 43 40
WWW.LEBRISTOLPARIS.COM

GARDEN PEA "GUACAMOLE" WITH OLIVE OIL VINAIGRETTE

LAURENT

[MODERN FRENCH] Set in the glorious Champs-Elysées gardens in a pale pink nineteenth-century former Louis XIV hunting lodge, Laurent is the sort of special restaurant that makes Paris Paris. Grand, timeless, and utterly romantic with a gorgeous (and rare) outdoor terrace shaded by chestnut trees, the captivating environs are matched by the upgraded classic French cuisine of Alain Pégouret, who ensures a meal is as much a feast for the eyes as it is for the taste buds. Root vegetable "rolls" with purées, seasoned aromatics, and spicy oils are plated to look like a painter's palette. Fresh and meaty morels luxuriate in a foam of sauce *poulette*. Ultra-tender cod cheeks are paired with artichokes and mushrooms, and the restaurant's classic spider crab bound in lobster jelly and topped with fennel cream are, promises one of our critics, dishes straight from heaven. Even dessert, perhaps a crispy "waffle" filled with almond milk cream and wild strawberries, perfectly captures the flavor of Paris. But for oenophiles, the 30,000-bottle wine cellar is reason enough to come. Ever professional, Director Philippe Bourguignon and Sommelier Patrick Lair make navigating the astounding selection a thoughtful and enlightening experience.

CRITICS' TIPS

Men should consider wearing a jacket to feel most comfortable; however, it is not required.

Opt for the terrace on warm summer nights.

Anticipate people-watching. This is a power-lunch spot for businessmen, politicians, and artists.

41 AVENUE GABRIEL
75008 PARIS, FRANCE
+33 (0)1 42 25 00 39
WWW.LE-LAURENT.COM

LACQUERED DUCK WITH RED BELL PEPPER, DATE LEAVES, AND COLOMBO-FLAVORED TURNIPS

PIERRE GAGNAIRE

[MODERN FRENCH] Critics have often used terms like "mad scientist" and "experimental" to describe famed chef Pierre Gagnaire, but the chef's own assessment might be the most apt. He compares his cooking to jazz, a fitting metaphor since he riffs on ingredients like a musician, with creativity that's both antic and endlessly brilliant. In his eponymous and serenely decorated Right Bank restaurant, Chef Gagnaire lets stellar ingredients command diners' attention. His sole with sea anemone, with its nuances of tone and flavor, is like an Impressionist painting of the sea, says one of our critics. Despite the many ingredients in his turbot entrée— leeks, codfish, juice of high-bush cranberries, and a tiny mackerel in anchovy sauce—another critic marvels at the chef's ability to bring the focus back to the firm, white-fleshed fish from Brittany. The menu changes with the seasons, but Gagnaire rarely does: always original, always seeking out new flavors and combinations. Eating food crafted by the man many critics consider the bravest, most exciting, and most original chef promises to be a revelation.

CRITICS' TIPS

Request the corner table in the back of the dining room or a table along the windows.

Gagnaire has long had a fondness for ramps, even before they were in fashion. If you visit in the spring, look for l'ail des ours *on the menu and order them.*

Don't miss the cheese course; Gagnaire has done away with the traditional cheese trolley and now serves a single, amazing plate of many different tastes.

HOTEL BALZAC PARIS
6 RUE BALZAC
75008 PARIS, FRANCE
+33 (0)1 58 36 12 50
WWW.PIERRE-GAGNAIRE.COM

SARDINE GELÉE BOUILLABAISSE WITH ROUILLE SAUCE

LE PRÉ CATELAN

[MODERN FRENCH] It's hard to top the romance of dining alfresco in Paris's Bois de Boulogne in springtime, although a table for two by a roaring fire on a chilly winter evening comes close. Chef Frédéric Anton, the first student of Joël Robuchon to rise to culinary superstardom, offers both in this stunning, marble-columned venue, along with his ever-inventive French cuisine and some of the best service in the city. Having championed market-driven fare before it was fashionable, Chef Anton has long organized his menus by ingredients—crab, foie gras, lamb, and more. As the diner, you need only decide on one main ingredient for the chef to present you with several variations to savor. Langoustines, for example, might appear in ravioli bathed in olive oil foam and perfumed with pepper and mint; as tempura with a smoky peanut sauce; and as a simply roasted masterpiece in coral butter with a cap of broccoli foam. Classic desserts, such as *Paris-Brest* and *tarte au citron*, seem nouvelle in the hands of Pastry Chef Chrystelle Brua, while Sommelier David Rivière has a retinue of wines to match every dish and occasion.

CRITICS' TIPS

Though hard to get, a terrace table is worth requesting during good weather, and fireside seats are prime during winter.

If you have any doubts about what to order, put yourself in the hands of Maître d'Hôtel Jean-Jacques Chauveau. His guidance is priceless.

Try anything with caviar or truffles; you are sure to be stunned.

BOIS DE BOULOGNE
ROUTE DE SURESNES
75016 PARIS, FRANCE
+33 (0)1 44 14 41 00
WWW.PRECATELANPARIS.COM

SAUTÉED FILLET OF RED MULLET, "SEEDS" OF CITRUS FRUIT AND
VEGETABLES, AND MARINATED SQUID

RESTAURANT GUY SAVOY

[FRENCH] Dubbed "one of the most creative and beloved chefs on the planet" by one of our critics, and a fixture on the Paris dining scene since his early 1980s debut in his then-"one-man-band," sixteenth arrondissement kitchen, Chef Guy Savoy is as known for stellar French cooking as he is for providing what many consider the best service in Paris. Singularly innovative, his food simultaneously bows to and transcends tradition. Case in point: Within his illustrious dining room he might present classic and meltingly moist roast *jarret de veau* (veal knuckle) followed by rectangles of shiny fresh salmon "cooked" tableside on a bed of dry ice by a waiter. Over the years Savoy has created a number of legendary signature dishes, including his modern French classic truffled artichoke soup accompanied with buttery truffled brioche and a refreshing interlude of tangy grapefruit terrine. (Never, ever turn it down, insists one critic.) Long before that, he was one of the first chefs to champion vegetables and to start working directly with growers. Today, his inventive menu still changes seasonally to highlight the freshest ingredients, and his expert staff help perfect the experience with guidance through the exceptional wine list.

CRITICS' TIPS

Be sure to confirm the address before you arrive. The restaurant is moving to the fifth arrondissement in 2013 or 2014, depending on construction.

If you reserve for lunch online, you are likely to secure a table—and enjoy a bargain price compared to dinner.

Try one of the two priced-fixed tasting menus; they're good ways to experience a wider variety of Savoy's outstanding cuisine.

18 RUE TROYON
75017 PARIS, FRANCE
+33 (0)1 43 80 40 61
WWW.GUYSAVOY.COM

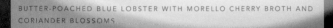
BUTTER-POACHED BLUE LOBSTER WITH MORELLO CHERRY BROTH AND
CORIANDER BLOSSOMS

RESTAURANT JEAN-FRANÇOIS PIÈGE

[MODERN FRENCH] Jean-François Piège's eponymous restaurant in the seventh arrondissement might best be described as tongue-in-chic. Its plush, midcentury furnishings and animal-skin throws invoke a Palm Springs speakeasy circa the Rat Pack era. Clearly, Piège is having fun. After a career that includes stints at Paris's Plaza Athénée and Hôtel de Crillon—not to mention on the television show *Top Chef*—Piège teamed with restaurateur Thierry Costes and interior designer India Mahdavi to create this 20-seat backdrop for what one critic calls "consistently provocative" cuisine. Daily menus, or *Règles du Je(u)*—rules of the game—offer five ingredients from which to choose as many as you wish, depending on price. Choices might include langoustines, beef, turbot, scallops, or lobster. Following an array of delightful appetizers, the fabulous langoustines might arrive with a pungent kaffir-lime-based sauce and a rectangle of perfectly seared foie gras. Carpaccio of beef is equally masterful with its classic crisscross of Parmesan cream. Spectacular cheese and dessert courses follow each seasonally based menu, and the remarkable wine list does justice to it all.

CRITICS' TIPS

Its small size makes reservations difficult to get. Call well in advance.

Ask Jean-François Piège about his passion for old culinary books—then let him decide what you eat and drink.

79 RUE SAINT-DOMINIQUE
75007 PARIS, FRANCE
+33 (0)1 47 05 49 75
WWW.THOUMIEUX.FR

LAMB TORTELLINI AND SEA URCHIN IN SARDINE AND ALGAE STOCK

RINO

[MEDITERRANEAN] Experience at the stoves of Paris's L'Arpège, Le Chateaubriand, and La Gazzetta paved the way for Chef Giovanni Passerini to reinvent bistro dining with this modern, relaxed "le fooding"-style restaurant. Tucked into a hip residential neighborhood behind the Bastille in the eleventh arrondissement, the restaurant's informal, cozy surroundings of wood tables, bright red banquettes, and matching light fixtures complement the mostly organic and extremely inventive cuisine. Light seasonal flavors and decidedly unfussy preparations are cornerstone to the series of set menus, which change daily based on availability and Chef Passerini's inspiration. Despite ongoing risk-taking in the kitchen, impressive training and innovative instincts mean that culinary missteps are rare. Dishes, such as sardine ravioli dotted with dill in fennel broth, Basque cod *pili pili* with aioli, and barley risotto with preserved lemon and fish eggs exemplify Passerini's ability to transform the familiar into the fantastic. Straightforward desserts— such as caramelized apple tart with fresh cream and hazelnuts or a *financièr* with blood orange ice cream—and a short but reasonably priced wine list of mainly organic or biodynamic Italian and French wines bookend a glorious meal.

CRITICS' TIPS

If you want to read reviews online, you can find links to a staggering number of them on Rino's website.

Sit at one of the high tables near the kitchen to watch the chefs in action.

Consider coming for lunch. It's an outrageous value for a restaurant of this quality.

46 RUE TROUSSEAU
75011 PARIS, FRANCE
+33 (0)1 48 06 95 85
WWW.RINO-RESTAURANT.COM

SECRETS OF THE SOMMELIER

We asked some of the world's top sommeliers for tips on navigating any wine list. From how to subtly express how much you'd like to spend to what not to pair with dessert, following are wine words to live by.

Price Consciousness
"Budget can be a delicate issue when looking at the wine list. You can always discreetly point to the area of the list where you feel comfortable with the prices. We understand."
—*Aldo Sohm, Le Bernardin, New York*

The Most Versatile Wine for Pairing
"Speaking in very general terms, if there is a table of four who all order different things, from lobster to beef, I would suggest a pinot noir. It's medium-bodied, and it pairs well with fish or meat." —*Bernard Sun, Jean-Georges, New York*

The Unsung Hero
"An overlooked wine that deserves more attention is Cru Beaujolais. There are some phenomenal producers that are making some incredible wines—Foillard, Breton, Lapierre, Sunier." —*Rajat Parr, Michael Mina, San Francisco*

Cheese-Course Companion
"Champagne I reserve for an aperitif and for cheese, not to build an entire meal around. With the rich fat of the cheese, the champagne gives you a fresh taste with personality. I especially like a pinot noir–dominated champagne."
—*Sylvain Nicolas, Restaurant Guy Savoy, Paris*

Poor Pairings
"Although I would not offer this information unless specifically asked, I think red wine is sometimes the worst pairing with cheese. The lactic of the cheese and the tannic structure of the wine do not combine well. But it's not wrong. It's always about individual and cultural preference."
—*Marco Pelletier, Epicure, Paris*

PEAR AND PARSLEY ICE CREAM WITH PINE NUTS AND
FOURME D'AMBERT

SATURNE

[MODERN FRENCH] Young chef Sven Chartier's restaurant featuring modern and gastronomic dishes reflects his Scandinavian and French heritage, Basque training, and time spent at Paris's L'Arpège and Racines restaurants. Inside, blonde wood, shell-shaped Serge Mouille–style sconces, and steel-buttressed skylights are reminiscent of a posh Scandinavian loft, while the menu answers diners' burgeoning desire for fresh, inventive fare that is simultaneously familiar and surprisingly new. Vegetables might be presented as if they were sheets of colorful pasta, full of integrity and flavor. Main courses are captivating, such as *cochon de lait* and fat slices of codfish; alabaster squid topped with tiny buckwheat blini; and moist and tender tarragon-kissed Sarthe-raised guinea fowl accompanied by grilled corn, shallot, and leek. The cheese course may feature particularly outstanding thick-crusted *pain des amis* from famed local baker Christophe Vasseur and perhaps thin slices of excellent Comté and Saint-Nectaire. In keeping with the contemporary, seasonally driven cuisine, Sommelier Ewen Lemoigne, who also hails from Racines, presides over a list of mostly natural, organic wines.

CRITICS' TIPS

Don't try to book a table on a weekend; the restaurant is closed on Saturday and Sunday.

For more diversity, consider coming for lunch, when there are three set menus compared to one during dinner.

If cochon de lait, *or baby pig, is on the menu, be sure to order it. It's succulent and memorable.*

17 RUE NOTRE-DAME DES VICTOIRES
75002 PARIS, FRANCE
+33 (0)1 42 60 31 90
WWW.SATURNE-PARIS.FR

RED RICE FLOUR ROLLS WITH SHRIMP

SHANG PALACE AT THE SHANGRI-LA HOTEL

O⊓

[CHINESE] Chef Frank Xu has set the bar high with his expertly prepared Chinese food. The resplendent and ornate interior created by a Hong Kong design team features lacquered woodwork, crystal chandeliers, gilded serving plates, and silver-plated chopstick rests—perfect ambassadors for Chinese culinary classics such as Peking duck, "lion's head" meatballs, wonton soup, and barbecued spareribs. A signature dish, Shang Palace rice is fried with egg, shrimp, chicken, Cantonese-style roasted duck, mushrooms, and seasonal vegetables steamed in a lotus leaf, which adds delicate aromatic notes. But it's the dim sum—which one of our critics describes as "elegant and ethereal, arriving in a kaleidoscope of colors, each little mouthful delivering surprise as well as pleasure"—that truly captivates. Of particular note are the shrimp-filled red rice flour rolls (pictured at left)—a Technicolor blend of red rice crepes enveloping a shrimp filling, anointed by thin bright green slices of raw asparagus. Scallop dumplings and feather-light barbecued pork buns also top the list. Service is flawlessly attentive and informed.

CRITICS' TIPS

Don't miss the mahogany-toned fried egg noodles, paired with shredded chicken and bean sprouts, or the crispy roast pig.

If you want Beggar's Chicken, a whole chicken in lotus leaf cooked in a clay pot, request it at least a day ahead, as it requires 24-hour advance notice.

Expect the dim sum menu only at lunch, and decide in advance if your party wants the fixed menu, which is only available to your whole party.

10 AVENUE D'IÉNA
75116 PARIS, FRANCE
+33 (0)1 53 67 19 92
WWW.SHANGRI-LA.COM/PARIS/SHANGRILA/
DINING/RESTAURANTS/SHANG-PALACE

CRISPY RED MULLET WITH EGGPLANT CAVIAR

LA TABLE D'AKI

[CONTEMPORARY FRENCH] In 2010, after working for 20 years under Bernard Pacaud at Paris's famed L'Ambroisie, Tokyo native and master *poissonnier* Akihiro Horikoshi opened his own tiny restaurant where he does it all with the assistance of just one server. As a result, the pure, simple, ultra-fresh food not only has the "Aki signature" but also the echo of Pacaud's sublime perfection. Within the 16-seat, light, white room with classic Thonet chairs, pendant lights, and a lively touch of red from lamp cables, a giant ravioli may arrive filled with sweet, fresh herb-dotted langoustines and served with a thin, potent meat sauce. Delicate, moist fricassée of chicken with carefully turned potatoes and baby onions tastes, according to one of our critics, "as though it were dropped from on high by the angels." The hallmark of Horikoshi's desserts is delicacy, executed perhaps in a silken crème caramel paired with an apple baked with a touch of cake inside or an ethereal *dacquoise* cake filled with raspberry cream.

CRITICS' TIPS

If you love seafood, come at night when the chef cooks only a fixed menu of delicacies from the sea.

Reserve well in advance; with so few seats, reservations are scarce.

When you arrive, prepare to be patient. Nothing moves fast here, but everything is marvelous and well worth the wait.

49 RUE VANEAU
75007 PARIS, FRANCE
+33 (0)1 45 44 43 48

ROASTED DUCK FOIE GRAS

TAILLEVENT

[FRENCH] Frequently acknowledged as the pinnacle of modern French haute cuisine, this monument to classic culinary perfection is as timeless and revered as the nearby Arc de Triomphe. A favorite choice for celebrations of all kinds, its understated clublike dining room within a nineteenth-century townhouse is cozy and contemporary with exposed oak paneling and modern art. The service, now under Jean-Marie Ancher, is the utmost in personal attention and care. Combined with the elegantly updated cuisine of Chef Alain Solivérès and Pastry Chef Sylvain Pétrel, everything is in place for a virtually flawless classic French dining experience. Dishes always employ the finest ingredients, and fish, shellfish, game, poultry, and meat are treated with the utmost respect, whether in the form of outstanding lobster *boudin*, an Asian-inspired lobster sausage in a delicate cream with a touch of caviar, crab rémoulade, or what one critic deems their "super-perfect chocolate tart." In winter months, black truffles reign, but the extensive wine list always stands out as one of the glories of the establishment.

CRITICS' TIPS

For larger parties, consider one of the two private dining rooms, which can accommodate groups from 6 to 32 people.

Dress accordingly; jackets are required for men.

Don't miss the vanilla mille-feuille. It's one of the lightest and flakiest in Paris.

15 RUE LAMENNAIS
75008 PARIS, FRANCE
+33 (0)1 44 95 15 01
WWW.TAILLEVENT.COM

STEAMED ROCKFISH WITH BLACK RICE

YAM'TCHA

[FRENCH-ASIAN FUSION] In a tiny, 24-seat space not far from Les Halles, Chef Adeline Grattard takes her classic French training due east, inflecting her cooking with influences from her husband's native Hong Kong. Exposed brick and beams make the cozy dining room seem a perfect setting for Chef Grattard's intimate cooking. The price-fixed tasting menu changes daily, wholly dependent on what the chef fancies at each morning's market. A veteran of Paris's L'Astrance restaurant before residing in Hong Kong, Grattard wields her wok to great effect in dishes such as roasted Challans duckling with Sichuan-style eggplant or crunchy Mozambique shrimp in spicy XO sauce with grated potatoes and dried prawns. Grattard's husband, Chi Wah Chan, acts as tea steward, pairing earthy, smoky, and sweet teas with each dish, including perhaps an *amuse* of slivered broad beans and pork sautéed with ginger, garlic, and sesame-seed oil. Grattard holds the French flag high during the cheese course, with a creamy, mild cheese from her birthplace, Chenôve, Burgundy. Her heritage shows clearly in the wine list as well, and desserts deliciously meld Eastern and Western sensibilities.

CRITICS' TIPS

Reserve well in advance, as both popularity and size limit the availability here.

Meals can run long. Expect to be here several hours.

Don't be afraid to sample the food-and-tea menu. You'll rarely find it anywhere else—and you could also drink wine with it if you prefer.

4 RUE SAUVAL
75001 PARIS, FRANCE
+33 (0)1 40 26 08 07
WWW.YAMTCHA.COM

RAZOR CLAMS WITH THAI BASIL, GREEN CURRY, AND SHELLFISH JUS

ZE KITCHEN GALERIE

[FRENCH-ASIAN FUSION] Many chefs combine Eastern and Western kitchen sensibilities and flavors, but few do it as creatively and successfully as William Ledeuil at Ze Kitchen Galerie. After making a name for himself at Paris's Bistrot de l'Etoile and Les Bouquinistes, Chef Ledeuil now combines his classical French training with a passion for all things Asian in his own loftlike space. The minimalist décor and contemporary art provide ideal backdrops for the fireworks Ledeuil creates in the kitchen. His wasabi and *tarama* with smoked tuna and *poutargue*—unforgettably strong and salty cured codfish eggs—sounds complex, but it is actually quite simple and surprising on the palate. Sea bass ravioli with capsicum-lemongrass condiment and shellfish broth is likely to be remembered long after the meal ends. Ledeuil also wrests flavor from produce, herbs, and spices with little added fat, creating a ginger-gooseberry seasoning as an impeccable accompaniment to confit of *Ibérique* pork. Imaginative combinations continue into dessert, perhaps in the form of white chocolate–wasabi ice cream topped with mango and mangosteen. As one of our critics rightly promises, "Flavors here are always enticing and always exciting."

CRITICS' TIPS

The kitchen is relatively open. To watch the chefs at work, ask for a table closer to the back.

Don't miss the art, which Chef Ledeuil rotates regularly (hence the "Galerie" in the restaurant name).

Be brave and go for the tasting menu. It's always delicious and always a treat.

4 RUE DES GRANDS-AUGUSTINS
75006 PARIS, FRANCE
+33 (0)1 44 32 00 32
WWW.ZEKITCHENGALERIE.FR

"PRESSED" AVOCADO AND MONKFISH

LA GRENOUILLÈRE

[Contemporary French] After growing up in his father's restaurant and working in establishments throughout France, Chef Alexandre Gauthier found his way back home—and made it his mission to revive his family's La Grenouillère in a small town outside of Calais. At the helm, he challenges and reinterprets traditional French cooking concepts with notably gastronomic, modern, and surprising results. Lobster may arrive tucked in a burning juniper branch. A "seawater" appetizer is literally salted water dressed up, perhaps, with green strawberries and cockles. Watercress ice cream with avocado illuminates Gauthier's ability to transcend the expected straight through the final course. A recent makeover by notable French designer and architect Patrick Bouchain infused a sense of postindustrial minimalism into the welcoming open-kitchen restaurant, while its riverside location in a three-centuries-old farmhouse, surrounded by lush gardens and rentable wooden huts as unique as Gauthier's dishes, gives even more reason to make a reservation and stay awhile.

CRITICS' TIPS

Arrive early and have a predinner cocktail in the quaint courtyard.

While in the area, consider visiting Gauthier's excellent rotisserie restaurant, Froggy's Tavern, which is five minutes away in the town of Montreuil.

19 RUE DE LA GRENOUILLÈRE
62170 LA MADELAINE-SOUS-MONTREUIL,
FRANCE
+33 (0)3 21 06 07 22
WWW.LAGRENOUILLERE.FR

"TWO MILLIMETERS" POLENTA AND BLACK TRUFFLE

FLOCONS DE SEL

[Contemporary French] Paris-trained Emmanuel Renaut, who launched his career in the restaurant within the Hôtel de Crillon and later became sous-chef to French molecular gastronomist Marc Veyrat, takes his modern French cuisine to great heights—literally— at his restaurant attached to a luxury resort in a popular ski area not far from Monte Blanc. Flanked by upscale lodges and soaring views of the French Alps, and adorned with a collection of cuckoo clocks, his dining room showcases the flavors of the region, with ingredients gathered from nearby markets, cheese shops, bakeries, distilleries, fishermen, beekeepers, and the natural surroundings. The menu, available both à la carte and as a fixed-price tasting selection, abounds with seafood options, many of which are fresh-caught from nearby Lake Geneva, as well as a stunning vegetable mille-feuille featuring fine leaves of carrot, celery root, potato, and other fresh vegetables mingled with *duxelles* (mushroom hash). The accompanying wine list is a tome that weighs heavy with French varietals. Desserts, such as ice-milk-filled meringue with stewed orange, lean toward light and refreshing.

CRITICS' TIPS

Reserve far in advance during winter, which is the region's high season.

Request a table near the window, which affords the best views of the celestial surroundings.

Consider taking one of Renaut's theme-based cooking classes, which are offered regularly.

1775 ROUTE DU LEUTAZ
74120 MEGÈVE, FRANCE
+33 (0)4 50 21 49 99
WWW.FLOCONSDESEL.COM

MONKFISH WITH BARBERRIES

MAISON TROISGROS

[MODERN FRENCH] The Troisgros name has been synonymous with fine French cuisine for more than 80 years for good reason. Current chef-proprietor Michel Troisgros is the third generation to successfully champion the family's legendary culinary heritage. After honing his craft both in France and abroad, he returned home to cook alongside his father and ultimately take the reins, now crafting cuisine that he describes as a playful mix of traditional French cooking with more experimental styles. The sprawling restaurant faces both a square named for Troisgros's late uncle, Jean, and a verdant garden. Inside, the serene dining room's vivid green dinnerware echoes the exterior. But even more vibrant is what appears on the plate, such as *mezzaluna de pomme de terre, parmesan et truffe*—half moons of pasta stuffed with potato, Parmesan, and black truffle, bathing in a butter mushroom sauce—or *saumon à l'oseille*, a decades-old standard of salmon fillet in a sorrel sauce accented with shallots and white wine. With more than 2,000 wines in the cellar and helpful guidance at the ready, finding an ideal dinner companion is effortless.

CRITICS' TIPS

Remember that the restaurant is closed for several weeks in late winter and late August.

Consider booking a room at the Troisgros hotel so your entire party can wholeheartedly explore the massive wine list.

PLACE DE LA GARE
42300 ROANNE, FRANCE
+33 (0)4 77 71 66 97
WWW.TROISGROS.FR

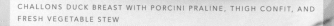

CHALLONS DUCK BREAST WITH PORCINI PRALINE, THIGH CONFIT, AND FRESH VEGETABLE STEW

RÉGIS ET JACQUES MARCON

[MODERN FRENCH] Perched atop a hill in the far reaches of France's south-central Haute-Loire, the hotel and restaurant of father-son chefs Régis and Jacques Marcon are well worth a detour. Both born and raised in the tiny village of Saint-Bonnet-le-Froid—and trained in the kitchen from an early age—they exhibit their long-standing passion for the best of the region's bounty through the use of fresh herbs, locally raised meats and poultry, lentils from neighboring Puy, and the cornerstone of Marcon cooking: freshly foraged mushrooms. The Marcons' way with fungi is renowned, and each morning's deliveries arrive from nearby forests. A tasting menu flaunts them to great advantage, perhaps in a fragrant *phô* of lobster and trumpet mushrooms with broth perfumed perfectly with freshly picked herbs. Intensely flavored and wonderfully tender lamb, served *en croute*, is also superb. Complementing the meal is a vast, heavily French wine list; a cheese board laden with wonderful choices from the Ardèche and Auvergne; and modern-minimalist décor that allows the views of the surrounding mountains to take center stage. Warm and professional, the service alone can make you glad you made the trip.

CRITICS' TIPS

Consider visiting in fall, when mushroom season is at its peak.

Be sure to reserve well in advance; the restaurant is closed midweek and during certain holiday periods.

If it's available, order the pineapple with morel caramel. It's a must.

LARSIALLAS
43290 SAINT-BONNET-LE-FROID, FRANCE
+33 (0)4 71 59 93 72
WWW.REGISMARCON.FR

TRUFFLE
FACTS & TIPS

Naturally grown amid the roots of many tree species in various parts of the world, sniffed out when ripe by trained dogs, and sold at astronomical prices to the world's top chefs and food lovers, the subterranean mushroom known as the truffle is the world's most elusive and expensive ingredient. You're sure to have opportunities to experience the truffle if you dine at some of the restaurants in this book, so consider this a primer on the most popular varieties and how to make good choices from menus with truffle offerings.

Black Truffles *(tuber melanosporum)*

The most versatile truffle with great culinary interest is the French black truffle. Primarily found in France, it grows with oak and hazel trees and has a harvest season from mid-November to March with quality peaking in January and February. Shaved onto dishes as an aromatic garnish, cut into matchsticks for texture, sliced, peeled, or even used whole, the black truffle is preferred by chefs because it can be served (lightly) cooked as well as raw, and refrigerated or frozen for future use, and still maintain flavor and aroma. (Although once frozen, its white "veins" will no longer be visible.)

White Truffles *(tuber magnatum)*

The white truffle, the best of which are known as the "Alba madonna," is the most expensive of truffle varieties. It grows symbiotically with oak, hazel, poplar, and beech trees, and its harvest begins in September, with a peak in October and completion in late December. Known for its steep price—often four to five times that of the French black truffle—and intense aroma, it is very delicate and must be enjoyed within a few days after its harvest, before it loses its character. Always served raw and primarily used for last-minute shavings atop light dishes, white truffles should never be heated, as they will instantly lose their flavor and aroma.

BLACK AND WHITE TRUFFLES

Truffle Menu Considerations

Take the advice of France-based Christopher Poron, owner of Plantin, one of the world's top truffle sources: When considering truffle-enhanced dishes, "Always look for a simple combination. Usually, the simpler it is, the better it is." For black truffles, exceptional food pairings include eggs, toasted bread with butter, cheese, risotto, pasta, scallops, langoustine, lobster, artichokes, asparagus, and sunchokes. For white truffles, look for light, simple preparations, especially those featuring pasta, eggs, or polenta.

Avoid dishes with extremely strong flavors, which will overpower the aroma of truffles.

Ask if the dish in question is made with fresh truffles or truffle oils. The latter is most often not made with truffles at all; instead the oil contains "synthetic" or "identical" aromas, which are added to impart the familiar and coveted aroma of truffles. While dishes made with truffle oil may be enjoyable, they should not demand the premium prices associated with dishes made with actual truffles.

When choosing wine, consider a selection from the region of the truffle's origin. For example, the French black truffle shines with whites and reds from the southern Rhône region—especially Châteauneuf-du-Papes—as well as delicate white Burgundies. Avoid intensely flavored wines, which overpower the delicate taste and aroma of truffles.

"ROTTEN" EGG WITH "MELANO" BLACK TRUFFLES ON WILD MUSHROOM AND TRUFFLE PURÉE WITH TRUFFLED BRIOCHE AND MUSHROOM CAPPUCCINO

AUBERGE DU VIEUX PUITS

[French] In a charming cottage located in a quaint mountain village of less than 150 inhabitants, Chef Gilles Goujon and his wife, Marie-Christine, exemplify the rustic, hearty character of French country cooking to perfection. So much so, in fact, that one critic describes the cuisine as "elegant stick-to-your-ribs food that perfectly expresses this chef's Rabelaisian style." One taste of the lobster with black ravioli featuring squid ink, squid, and bell pepper coulis proves the point. Goujon's brilliance is further evident in his deconstructed take on traditional southern French and Languedocian fare, such as the roasted free-range pork with green olives and a jus of roasting juices served with butter-roasted potatoes and a purée of boudin noir and potato. The menu is heavy on seafood, so expect salmon roe, caviar, oysters, and other fruits from the sea. No true French meal is complete without one serious cheese course, so take heed and save room. While you're here, consider booking a room at their auberge so you can arrive early, spend the day in Fontjoncouse, then reward yourself with a memorable meal.

CRITICS' TIPS

Plan your visit for late summer or early fall, as both the local produce and the local scenery are unparalleled during these seasons.

Don't miss the oeuf pourri au truffes, Goujon's famous egg dish whereby the yolk is poached separately from the white, the white is seasoned with truffles, and the shell is filled with a purée of truffles and wild mushrooms before the egg is reassembled.

Get to know Goujon's talents through the more-affordable Bienvenue au Pays menu served only during weekday lunch.

5 AVENUE SAINT-VICTOR
11360 FONTJONCOUSE, FRANCE
+33 (0)4 68 44 07 37
WWW.AUBERGEDUVIEUXPUITS.FR

THE FAMED "GARGOUILLOU" VEGETABLE ENSEMBLE

BRAS

[Modern French] After growing up in his parents' rural café and exploring every last forest and brook in the Aubrac countryside, self-taught chef Michel Bras opened this eponymous restaurant, which he now runs with his son Sébastien. Today, Sébastien maintains the status his father garnered as "the master of *cuisine terroir*" as well as one of the world's most revered chefs, elevating everyday herbs, flowers, and vegetables from his bucolic surroundings into shockingly pure yet refined regional dishes that astonish, delight, and accentuate a true sense of place. While meat and fish are done beautifully here, it's their accompanying vegetables that truly awe, perhaps in the form of heirloom tomatoes transformed into seasoned, colorful tubes or his famed *le gargouillou* vegetable plate, which combines dozens of individually prepared vegetables, flowers, and seeds plated with artistry and purpose. Ironically, his best-known creation is molten chocolate cake, which has been replicated in kitchens worldwide. As masters at concentrating flavors and elevating them with added and unexpected "shocks to the palate," the father-and-son duo exhibit a culinary vision as transcendent as their tasteful, ultramodern dining room with its panoramic views of the *plateau de l'Aubrac*.

CRITICS' TIPS

Plan your visit wisely; the restaurant is only open April through October.

Follow the French and dine late—then fall into a satiated slumber at Bras's adjoining auberge.

ROUTE DE L'AUBRAC
12210 LAGUIOLE, FRANCE
+33 (0)5 65 51 18 20
WWW.BRAS.FR

QUINOA RISOTTO, MORELS, AND PARMESAN CREAM

MIRAZUR

[Modern Mediterranean] Italo-Argentinian Mauro Colagreco doesn't merely offer picture-perfect views of the sea and marina in his four-level, 1930s-style restaurant perched on a hillside on the French-Italian border near Monaco; the highly acclaimed chef presents a modern taste of the surroundings. Despite his South American origins, his creative menu is decidedly French with Mediterranean and molecular gastronomic influences, making use of local fruits, vegetables, herbs, and flowers from his garden and his experience at the Côte d'Or under the late Bernard Loiseau, at Paris's famed L'Arpège with Alain Passard, and Plaza Athénée with Alain Ducasse. The ever-changing menu, which is entirely dictated by the day's fresh finds, might feature morels with potato purée foam, sweet miniature broad beans, and a flourish of chive flowers, or deconstructed roast lamb with grilled onions and artichokes, tapenade, lamb jus, and herbs. While vegetable dishes are a focus, local meats and seafood have their own shining moments. Case in point: The signature minimally grilled and naturally sweet San Remo red prawns—impeccably prepared, artfully plated, and garnished with wild strawberries and flavorful petals of borage, fennel, hyssop, and yarrow—is a dream dish served in environs that perfectly encapsulate the breathtaking allure of the Mediterranean.

CRITICS' TIPS

If you want a bargain, the midweek fixed-price lunch menu is the most approachable option. It also provides the opportunity to enjoy a long, lazy afternoon with one of the best views around.

Take the time to explore the restaurant's vegetable garden, as well as its herb and citrus-fruit garden.

30 AVENUE ARISTIDE BRIAND
06500 MENTON, FRANCE
+33 (0)4 92 41 86 86
WWW.MIRAZUR.FR

SHELLFISH, OCTOPUS, AND SQUID WITH *ROUGIERS* CHICKPEAS

LE LOUIS XV

[MODERN GASTRONOMIC FRENCH] The restaurant within Monaco's opulent Hôtel de Paris, Le Louis XV is food legend Alain Ducasse's flagship restaurant. Here co-Chefs Franck Cerutti and Dominique Lory use their proximity to the Mediterranean Sea and Provence to execute Ducasse's flamboyant sophisticated style of modern French cuisine. The freshest of seafood dishes can be found here, perhaps presented as a stew of stockfish tripe with salt cod, Perugina sausage, and lettuce with lemon sauce. But heartier and perfectly prepared meat offerings, such as suckling pig, also grace the menu. Fitting Monaco's extravagant environs and clientele, a 400,000-bottle wine cave ensures no oenophile request goes unrequited, while Ducasse's famed dessert cart is impossible to resist, even after indulging in his trademark *Baba au Rhum*—a sweet cake painted with vanilla, orange, and lemon glazes and finished with whipped vanilla cream and your choice of rum. Like the restaurant's namesake, the neo-Baroque-style, gold-tinged Le Louis XV is fit for royalty, inspiring one of our critics to declare it "the most gorgeous interior in the world, with elegant service to match."

CRITICS' TIPS

If possible, dine here in spring when the largest variety of fresh, local ingredients is available.

Request a table on the left-hand side of the far end of the restaurant for a view of the entire space.

Dress accordingly; jackets are required.

HÔTEL DE PARIS
PLACE DU CASINO
9800 MONTE-CARLO, MONACO
+377 98 06 88 64
WWW.ALAIN-DUCASSE.COM/EN/RESTAURANT/
LE-LOUIS-XV-ALAIN-DUCASSE

JAPAN

HAY-ROASTED PIGEON WITH WHEAT AND BURNED BREAD RISOTTO, BEETS, AND BLACK CURRANT

ESQUISSE

[MODERN FRENCH] Less than a year old, this French fine-dining establishment helmed by Frenchman and former Maison Troisgros chef Lionel Beccat has already established itself as one of Tokyo's top restaurants. Tucked away on the seventh floor of a Ginza district high-rise, the intimate dining room with its neutral pastel walls, wood beam ceilings, and oversize windows is a peaceful refuge for enjoying Beccat's daily changing tasting menus. As the name suggests ("esquisse" means drawing), the daily *menu spontané* begins as rough sketches based on seasonally available ingredients that are transformed into visually arresting works of art as original as the hand-thrown plateware they're served on. Like an expert watercolorist, Beccat blends Japanese ingredients with French techniques to create dishes such as a summer consommé with duck bouillon in which the dried duck meat is used like dried bonito to enrich the broth. Desserts are also a delightful surprise of compositions, flavors, and presentations. Appropriately for a French restaurant located in Japan, guests can opt to pair their meal with fine wine or a pot of freshly steeped tea.

CRITICS' TIPS

For maximum privacy, request a table for two by the window or the private room that can accommodate small groups.

For a lighter, less-expensive meal, come for the fixed-price lunch.

If you love wine, ask Sommelier Eiji Wakabayashi for a suggestion. The list is full of grand vins from Bourgogne and fine vintages from Bordeaux.

ROYAL CRYSTAL GINZA 9F
5-4-6 GINZA, CHUO-KU, TOKYO 104-0061
+81 3 5537 5580
WWW.ESQUISSETOKYO.COM

FOIE GRAS PICKLED IN SAKE LEES

GENTOUSHI NAKADA

[JAPANESE] Not strictly a members-only restaurant but pretty close, this Japanese gem hidden in the quiet basement of an ordinary condominium is hard to get into, especially since it offers only one seating a night and has a mere six seats at a counter and a single private dining room. However, it's worth the effort because each night Chef-Proprietor Noboru Nakada treats guests to his extremely unique and unforgettable interpretation of Japanese cuisine. Leveraging an unexpectedly diverse selection of ingredients and his past experience as a chef of French cuisine, Chef Nakada artfully balances Japanese and European cooking techniques and a less-is-more aesthetic to craft his seasonally appropriate Japanese fare. Consequently, you might find a consommé with local *ayu* fish in summer or whole black truffle tempura in the fall. Though deceptively simple in appearance, his dishes achieve exemplary results through meticulous and often time-consuming preparations, as is the case with his trademark dish, foie gras pickled in the lees of sake. It's the quintessence of Japanese food on a plate, a revelation that tastes even better paired with a glass of platinum Masuizumi sake.

CRITICS' TIPS

To secure a reservation, rather than calling directly, ask a concierge from a luxury hotel to book a table on your behalf.

Don't miss the foie gras Kasuzuke. It's the perfect marriage of French ingredients and traditional Japanese culinary technique.

Look for seafood from Hokuriku, the chef's hometown, which is along the northwestern part of Japan's main island.

ARISUGAWA NATIONAL COURT B1F
2-1-20 MOTO-AZABU, MINATO-KU, TOKYO 106-0046
+81 90 4228 3817

SEA URCHIN AND WAKAME SEAWEED OVER SEASONED STEAMED RICE

ISHIKAWA

[JAPANESE KAISEKI] In a black wood building tucked behind Tokyo's Bishamonten shrine, Chef Hideki Ishikawa has created a temple of his own, one that reveres superior service as highly as it does Japanese *kaiseki*. Ishikawa elevates the traditional, multicourse Japanese dinner, but he does so without fanfare. The spare, modern dining room holds just four tables and seven seats at a counter made of century-old Japanese cypress. Ishikawa oversees everything himself, using only what's in season to craft his ever-changing set menu, often answering guests' questions and presenting the dishes he has lovingly prepared. Every one of his kimono-clad servers can tell you the provenance of your meal; they may even go to the extent of producing an encyclopedia to illustrate unusual ingredients, such as those in a starter of conger eel with cucumber, *myoga* ginger, and a sauce of egg yolk and white radish, or tempura-fried *ankimo* (monkfish liver) and lotus roots. The meal-ending rice veers from the simple norm, rich with stock and matsutake mushrooms, risotto-like in its richness. Wine and sake offerings perfectly complement the inspired cuisine.

CRITICS' TIPS

Don't hesitate to ask for details on mystery ingredients. The staff goes out of their way to help educate diners.

Don't feel required to finish the finale rice dish. The restaurant will pack the leftovers for you to take home, and it tastes just as good the next day.

Don't be surprised if Hideki Ishikawa recognizes you on a return visit— or makes sure you don't have any of the same dishes a second time. His memory and attention to detail are astounding.

TAKAMURA BUILDING 1F
5-37 KAGURAZAKA, SHINJUKU-KU, TOKYO 162-0825
+81 3 5225 0173
WWW.KAGURAZAKA-ISHIKAWA.CO.JP

GRILLED JAPANESE SPINY LOBSTER WITH WHITE MISO SAUCE

[JAPANESE] No one knows Kyoto cuisine better than Masao Ueda. The thoroughbred of the Japanese chefs, he was born into a Kyoto family that's long run one of the top traditional local *ryokans* (traditional inns) and boasts decades of experience in Japan's famous restaurants, including Tokyo's Kyo Aji under well-known Chef Kenichiro Nishi and one of Kyoto's Wakuden locations. At this traditional establishment Chef Ueda leverages his experience and skill to blend Eastern and Western cooking techniques into a truly spectacular and wholly original dining experience. Classic Kyoto dishes are still the focus, but they are heavily infused with Tokyo influence. Prepared from the finest seasonal ingredients, dishes might include inspired renditions of *hamo shabu-shabu* (pike eel that you cook in a small pot of hot broth), thinly sliced Kyoto-style matsutake—mushrooms similarly cooked in broth at the table—or *ebi-imo*, a skinned and fried variety of taro root common in Kyoto cuisine that is anything but everyday in Chef Ueda's expert hands. The amiable service of Ueda's wife, who boasts an impressive knowledge of wines, can assist with a selection that best complements her husband's thoughtful cuisine.

CRITICS' TIPS

Because this restaurant caters to a dedicated recurring clientele, it does not take reservations for first-time visitors; to get in the door find a regular customer who will take you as a guest or ask your concierge for help.

Try securing a later dinner reservation; it is sometimes possible to get in after 9 p.m., however you may still need the assistance of a regular customer or your concierge.

SUNRITTO GINZA BUILDING 1F
5-14-15 GINZA, CHUO-KU, TOKYO 104-0061
+81 3 5550 2022

SCORPION FISH SASHIMI

KANDA

[JAPANESE KAISEKI] Proprietor Hiroyuki Kanda garnered years of experience in world-class kitchens in France and Japan before opening his highly celebrated *kaiseki* hidden behind an unmarked door in a residential apartment building near Roppongi Station. Though his sushi den, replete with a mere eight-seat wood-lined counter and a single small private dining room, isn't easy to find, regulars and first-timers agree it's worth seeking, especially since (unlike many notable sushi establishments) Chef Kanda welcomes foreigners with the same enthusiasm as he does Japanese regulars. True to *kaiseki* style, the contemporary Japanese cuisine is presented in an ever-changing set-course menu, guided by the season and the chef's inspiration. But it always consists of a series of raw and cooked dishes presented with a simple aesthetic that belies the kitchen's exacting efforts. The offerings might include buttery beef cheeks, a sublime *kawahagi* (finfish) sashimi with liver, or a featherlike fried *ayu* (sweetfish) tempura. Pair the meal with premium sake or let the sommelier help choose something from the extensive wine list, which includes an impressive selection of European wines.

CRITICS' TIPS

It's easy to miss the entranceway of this nondescript building. Look for the small sign that bears two Japanese characters, which spell out the restaurant's name.

To fully experience the chef's talents, splurge for the most expensive of the three tasting menus that your budget allows.

If you'd like a kaiseki-style experience whereby conversation with the staff is part of the experience, come here. The staff speak English and are happy to share information.

KA-MU MOTO-AZABU 1F
3-6-34 MOTO-AZABU, MINATO-KU, TOKYO 106-0046
+81 3 5786 0150
WWW.NIHONRYORI-KANDA.COM

JAPANESE WAGYU CHATEAUBRIAND

KAWAMURA

[JAPANESE STEAKHOUSE] With only eight seats at a small counter and reservations often booked up seven months in advance, Kawamura is one of the most difficult reservations to get in Tokyo. But there's another reason, too: Chef Taro Kawamura's way with Japanese beef is not only renowned, it's virtually unparalleled. "A magician," one critic calls Kawamura, who uses low temperatures rather than high heat to produce beef so tender it will slice under the weight of your knife. Kawamura does everything here, from smoking salmon for appetizers to making his own foie gras paté to selecting the cuts of Kobe and *wagyu* beef, which he grills for more than an hour and "rests" multiple times along the way to coax maximum flavor from each bite. Dishes, which are entirely seasonal and varied, change often, and there is no menu. Kawamura simply lists what's available and, after some discussion, creates an entirely personalized meal. However, some offerings remain relatively constant, including a beef consommé (pictured at left) that repeatedly earns raves despite its seeming simplicity. A superb starter of abalone in sour cream sauce might be the high point in a lesser restaurant. Here, it's an excellent prelude to the headlining steak: perfectly cooked to your preference, impossibly tender, and intensely flavorful.

CRITICS' TIPS

Reservations are exceedingly difficult to secure since new diners must be introduced by a regular customer. Recruit the help of a concierge from a top-quality hotel and try for a table around 5 p.m. or after 11 p.m.

Take a tip from regulars and order a hamburger to take home. It makes an excellent breakfast the next morning.

Don't leave the restaurant without ordering pudding for dessert. It's so good it deserves a storefront of its own.

TOUGO BUILDING 1F
7-3-16 GINZA, CHUO-KU, TOKYO 104-0061
+81 3 3289 8222

JAPANESE CUISINE GLOSSARY

There's more to describing the traditional cuisine of Japan than "Japanese food." In fact, restaurants around the country usually specialize in a specific type of Japanese cuisine, a single star ingredient, or a style of service, each done with a level of expertise that can only be achieved through focused, wholehearted commitment. Understanding the following terms will prove useful when reading this guide and dining throughout Japan.

bento: A meal usually served for lunch or as a to-go option with a variety of dishes served in a traditional, multicompartment box

kaiseki: Originally a ritual meal served prior to a Zen tea ceremony, now a formal multicourse meal of small portions featuring delicate flavors, seasonal ingredients, and artful presentation

kappo: Japanese fine dining with counter seating where the chef prepares some or all of the food in front of you

Kyo-ryōri: Kyoto-style food known for its distinct sophistication, visual beauty, and subtlety of taste

nigiri sushi: A piece of raw or cooked fish, vegetable, meat, or egg hand-placed on top of a bite-size portion of seasoned white rice

maki sushi: A sushi "roll," in which dried seaweed is wrapped around fish, other ingredients, and seasoned white rice

omakase: Literally "chef's choice," a multicourse meal in which all the selections are made by the chef

ryōtei: A luxurious and generally very expensive small restaurant focused on formal seasonal cuisine

sashimi: Very thinly sliced pieces of raw fish

shabu-shabu: Meat and vegetables cooked at the table in clear soup broth or dashi in "hot-pot" style

tempura-ya: A restaurant serving battered, quickly fried vegetables and seafood

COMMON SUSHI, SASHIMI, AND FISH

aji—horse mackerel or jack mackerel

anago—saltwater eel or conger eel

ankimo—monkfish liver

ayu—sweetfish (a member of the trout family)

ebi—shrimp

fugu—puffer fish or blowfish

hamachi—young yellowtail tuna or amberjack

hamo—pike conger eel

hotate—scallop

ika—squid

ikura—cured salmon roe

maguro—tuna

saba—mackerel

suzuki—sea bass

tai—snapper

tako—octopus

tamago—sweet egg cake or omelet

tobiko—flying fish roe

toro—fatty tuna belly

uni—sea urchin

GIZZARD SHAD *NIGIRI*

KOZASA

[JAPANESE SUSHI] Not to be confused with Kozasa zushi in the Ginza district, this unmarked nine-seat sushi bar hidden down an alley has a devout food-connoisseur following for one simple reason: Chef Shigeki Sasaki does not compromise. Whether securing only the best catch of the day at the Tsukiji fish market or personally handcrafting and presenting every morsel, the modest proprietor-chef tirelessly works to maintain his tiny restaurant's reputation for exceptional sushi that, through minimal intervention, highlights the excellence of the fish. His simple, unadorned counter-only dining area, and the silence in which he crafts *nigiri* or grills a fatty piece of amberjack, leaves the focus entirely on the fish, all of which is fresh, never frozen. However, Chef Sasaki welcomes discussion around his cuisine and ingredients as he composes, perhaps, his trademark Aomori tuna, conger eel, or yellowtail, all considered by some of our critics beyond comparison. Among many other dishes, the seared-mackerel sushi, a Sasaki original, is reward enough for the difficult effort of securing a reservation. While sushi traditionally is served with green tea or beer, Sasaki broadens the minds of even the most conventional diners by offering Higan—a sake from the northwest coast of Honshu, which pairs unusually well with sushi.

CRITICS' TIPS

With so few seats, it isn't easy to get reservations here. Be persistent and ask for openings before or after the traditional dinner hour.

Get directions before you come; tucked in a residential neighborhood and bearing no sign outside, the location can be hard to find.

If you want superior Tokyo sushi at nearly half the price of better-known Ginza restaurants, this is the place to try.

10-12 SHINSEN-CHO, SHIBUYA-KU,
TOKYO 150-0045
+81 3 5458 2828

A SEASONAL VEGETABLE APPETIZER

KYO AJI

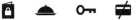

[JAPANESE] Run by the legendary chef Kenichiro Nishi, Kyo Aji is indisputably Tokyo's top traditional Japanese restaurant, offering the penultimate rendition of Kyoto-style *kappo* cuisine. Though the Shinbashi-neighborhood destination has been sought-after for decades and only one menu is offered a day, no meal is ever alike, as offerings change according to what's available in the market. But you can always count on superb ingredients and unusual delicacies, such as *hamo* (pike eel), painstakingly prepared and presented in dishes that match color and season. Wherever you sit, be it in the simple, 20-seat shoji-screen-lined room or at the blonde-wood counter where devotees vie to watch Chef Nishi in action, great attention is paid to the diner, from the presentation of the perennial favorite *harasu gohan*—rice topped with salmon belly—to the final made-to-order *kudzukiri* (cold kudzu dessert noodles) served in sweet syrup. The biggest challenge to enjoying a meal at Kyo Aji is similar to that at many of Tokyo's finest: It doesn't take reservations from first-time customers, so you'll need to be invited by a regular to secure a seat.

CRITICS' TIPS

Before you go, check out one of Mr. Nishi's many cookbooks to get a better sense of the man and his cuisine.

Request a seat at the counter where, if you're lucky, Chef Nishi will reveal to you the ins and outs of how he crafts his nightly meals.

Try to visit in the fall, when the kitchen serves its trademark hamo matsutake nabe, *sliced* hamo *and matsutake mushrooms cooked in a hot pot with dashi (broth).*

3-3-5 SHINBASHI, MINATO-KU,
TOKYO 105-0004
+81 3 3591 3344

SILLAGINOID FISH, JAPANESE TIGER PRAWN, AND
ASPARAGUS TEMPURA

MIKAWA ZEZANKYO

[JAPANESE TEMPURA] Tokyo may be rife with tempura houses, but Mikawa Zezankyo, the third outpost of Chef Tetsuya Saotome, stands apart. Filled with art and pottery commissioned by National Living Treasure artists, European antiques, and a giant copper ceiling fan in the shape of Saotome's trademark hat, the four-floor converted home is a virtual museum of tempura, where meticulous attention is paid to everything from the type of oil and ingredients used to the final presentation and tableware. Despite the lavish, eccentric décor, the focal point is undoubtedly the nine-seat L-shaped counter where diners can watch the chef at his artisanal best, as he listens to the sound of the oil and changes the frying time and temperature according to each ingredient. The degustation menu changes daily and showcases a procession of seasonal, locally available fish and vegetables fried to perfection. A shining example is the trademark *anago* (conger eel)—crispy on the outside, tender on the inside. According to one of our critics, it's the one and only authentic rendition of tempura made just the way it should be.

CRITICS' TIPS

Each season has its own set of signature dishes, but if you're lucky enough to visit in autumn, make sure to have the splendid matsutake mushroom tempura.

You can request to sit at one of the downstairs tables or in one of the small private tatami rooms upstairs, but the best seats in the house are at the chef's counter on the first floor.

If you're an art lover, leave time at the end of your meal to look around upstairs in the tearoom, which is filled with Saotome's private collection of sculpture, paintings, and ceramics.

1-3-1 FUKUZUMI, KOTO-KU,
TOKYO 135-0032
+81 3 3643 8383
MIKAWA-ZEZANKYO.JIMDO.COM/
ENGLISH-INFORMATION

MATSUBA CRAB *SHABU-SHABU*

RYUGIN

[JAPANESE] A meal at RyuGin offers diners the chance to taste ultramodern gourmet Japanese fare. While Chef Seiji Yamamoto was known for exploring Spanish molecular gastronomy in his younger days, the cuisine presented in his surprisingly casual 20-seat Roppongi Station restaurant has matured into well-executed, brilliantly conceived Japanese dishes. The tasting menus still employ cutting-edge cooking science, but they now also take direct inspiration from traditional seasonal *kaiseki* menus. The modest setting of dark wood tables and wall-mounted plates featuring dragon motifs belies the kitchen's sophistication. Culinary mastery is evident in everything from the head-to-tail presentation of Chef Yamamoto's signature charcoal grilled *ayu* (sweetfish) to the desserts, an area of specialty not often associated with Japanese cuisine. The chef's famous Minus-196 Degrees Candy Apple is a brilliant confection filled with nitrogen-chilled apple-flavored powder ice cream that's cracked open at the table and served with hot apple compote. It's the perfect finale to the kind of meal that professional cooks and avid foodies seek out when they want to enjoy food as entertainment.

CRITICS' TIPS

If you want to try the tasting menu, book two months in advance. Or drop in or make same-day reservations for the à la carte menu, which is offered after 9:30 p.m.

If you would like to enjoy an especially leisurely dinner, reserve the restaurant's private dining room.

If available, don't pass up the conger eel kabayaki. *Yamamoto famously requested a CT-scan of an eel to study its bone structure. The result is the softest, most elegant boneless eel dish that you will ever taste.*

SIDE ROPPONGI BUILDING 1F
7-17-24 ROPPONGI, MINATO-KU, TOKYO 106-0032
+81 3 3423 8006
WWW.NIHONRYORI-RYUGIN.COM

TORO NIGIRI

SUKIYABASHI JIRO

[JAPANESE SUSHI] Hailed as a natural treasure, the 86-year-old sushi master Jiro Ono, immortalized in the documentary *Jiro Dreams of Sushi,* is as busy as ever in his eponymous Ginza district restaurant. Considered by some as the *ne ultra plus* of sushi temples, not only in Tokyo but in the world, it's sequestered in the basement of an office building. Nevertheless, the 10-seat counter-only *sushi-ya* is sought after by legions of fans clamoring to watch Chef Ono turn out dish after dish of gleaming cuts of fish draped over still-warm, perfectly seasoned rice at breakneck speed. The ultratraditional sushi-dedicated *omakase* menu varies according to what's in season, but favorites include a trio of tuna (lean, medium fatty, and extra fatty) briefly marinated in soy sauce and crispy bonito skin roasted with rice straw that's redolent with a smoky aromatic flavor. A meal here is fast and furious—30 minutes perhaps for the entire 20-course menu—before guests are escorted to a side table to enjoy a slice of perfectly ripe melon (and thus make room for the next wave of diners). For many foodies, it's a dream come true.

CRITICS' TIPS

If you don't make a reservation a month in advance (accepted on the first day of each month), go directly to the restaurant and reserve any open seat by paying a reservation fee.

Plan when to come wisely: Insiders insist the best time to dine is 1 p.m. for lunch and 7 p.m. for dinner. These are the last seatings for each service, which ensures you'll be the only guests left in the room and will get Ono's undivided attention.

Bring plenty of yen; the restaurant is cash only.

TSUKAMOTO SOGYO BUILDING B1F
4-2-15 GINZA, CHUO-KU, TOKYO 104-0061
+81 3 3535 3600
WWW.SUSHI-JIRO.JP

JAPANESE HORSE MACKEREL *NIGIRI* WITH GINGER AND CHIVES

SUSHI NAKAMURA

[JAPANESE SUSHI] With its unobtrusive exterior—there's not even a name on the door—and its discreet location on a small, quiet street in the Roppongi area, it would be easy to miss Sushi Nakamura. Don't. In this narrow space behind sliding shoji doors, an exceptional experience awaits. While seated at one of a dozen stools at the honed-cedar bar, you can sip sake and watch Chef Masanori Nakamura and his assistants perform veritable sushi-making magic. Whether plating what is likely to be the best *ankimo* (monkfish liver) you'll ever taste or scoring *aji* (horse mackerel, pictured at left) with a sharp blade to create *nigiri* that is nothing short of edible art, their skillful movements mesmerize. There is no menu here, though you won't wish for one. Chef Nakamura serves only what's in season and fresh that day, and that might mean more than a dozen different kinds of seafood in a given meal. With deft motions and expertly applied seasonings, the chef makes each course soar, whether it's simple but exquisitely fresh tuna, salmon, or *uni* (sea urchin). The combination of supple texture and bracing flavors proves astonishing, particularly in contrast to the traditional, rather humble surroundings.

CRITICS' TIPS

Nakamura is closed on weekends, so plan accordingly.

Whatever you do, don't miss the tamago. *A dish that sushi connoisseurs often judge restaurants by, the impossibly light cake-like slice served here is a revelation.*

Sip your way through the sake list. It's concise but has more than enough excellent options.

YONEKYU BUILDING NO.2 1F
7-17-16 ROPPONGI, MINATO-KU, TOKYO 106-0032
+81 3 3746 0856

ABALONE AND OCTOPUS SASHIMI

SUSHI SAITO

[JAPANESE SUSHI] Despite its humble appearance and locale, Sushi Saito—a sparsely decorated seven-seat counter-only *sushi-ya* tucked away in an Akasaka office building parking lot next to the American Embassy—is one of Tokyo's best. Once through the entryway's red curtains, diners are rewarded with exquisite sushi sliced to order with ninja precision by the young and surprisingly gregarious chef Takashi Saito behind the counter. Lauded for its amazingly pristine Tsukiji fish market seafood (especially purple sea urchin, shellfish, and tuna) and rice perfectly seasoned with red rice vinegar and sea salt, Saito makes it impossible to order wrong. But the best way to experience the chef's masterful balance of taste, texture, and temperature is to simply order the *omakase* (chef's choice) menu, which always begins with appetizers and sashimi and ends with miso soup, tuna rolls, and *tamago*. Along the way, you'll shell out a lot of yen, but you will be entertained by the chef's knife-wielding wizardry and friendly banter. In true *sushi-ya* spirit, a small selection of sake and wine is available to pair with the meal.

CRITICS' TIPS

If you can't get a reservation, call several times in the early evening on the day you want to go; sometimes the restaurant gets cancellations.

If you can go during the day, the lunch menu is a fantastic deal, at about one-third of what you'll pay at dinner.

Don't be afraid to chat up the chef; Saito-san is charming, speaks some English, and is welcoming to first-timers and non-Japanese-speaking foreigners.

JITENSHA KAIKAN ICHIGO-KAN BUILDING 1F
1-9-15 AKASAKA, MINATO-KU, TOKYO 107-0052
+81 3 3589 4412

BONITO AND SPANISH MACKEREL SUSHI

SUSHISO MASA

[JAPANESE SUSHI] Tucked in the basement of a Nishiazabu office building, the Japanese *sushi-ya* Sushiso Masa is one of the best-kept secrets in Tokyo. Although the seven-seat destination has all the trappings of better-known sushi temples—no printed menu, counter seats only, and a showman sushi master—it's a personal favorite of insiders and critics who consider it more welcoming, more leisurely in pace, and a better value than its contemporaries. Presided over by Chef-Owner Masakatsu Oka and his assistants, the seafood-centric *omakase* meal consists of the freshest and best cuts of seasonal fish. The focal point and source of amazement remains squarely on the meal, which is prepared directly in front of guests, with no visual distractions. The chef is especially known for his deft preparation of more than 40 different kinds of fish, particularly white fish, which appear both raw and lightly grilled like a culinary fugue compelling diners to revisit their essence again and again. That attention to detail extends down to the service; despite the fact that no English is spoken, the level of hospitality you'll encounter here is as high as any luxury hotel.

CRITICS' TIPS

Reservations must be made by phone in advance, so you'll need to employ the help of a Japanese-speaking friend or a hotel concierge.

Feel free to bring out your camera; photographing is not frowned upon.

Masa stays open relatively late, so if you can't get a reservation, drop in around 10 p.m. to see if seats have become available.

SEVEN NISHIAZABU B1F
4-1-15 NISHIAZABU, MINATO-KU,
TOKYO 106-0031
+81 3 3499 9178

A SEASONAL FALL APPETIZER

GÔRA KADAN

[JAPANESE KAISEKI] Located two hours from Tokyo in Hakone National Park in a stately half-timbered mansion that was once the summer palace of the imperial family, Gôra Kadan is one of Japan's most exclusive *ryokans* (traditional Japanese inns). Although the rich and famous come to this mountain retreat to take the waters (Gôra is a well-known natural hot springs spa for healing), foodies make the trek for the world-class *Kyo-ryōri* (Kyoto-style) *kaiseki* dinners by Chef Makoto Kobayashi. The ever-changing procession of delicate appetizers, stellar sashimi, and alternating hot and cold dishes is presented like *ikebana* (the art of Japanese flower arranging) in beautiful ceramics and lacquerware and designed to reflect the beauty of the season. Menu highlights might include *yuba nabe* (a soy-milk cream in soy-milk broth), *yudofu* (tofu in dashi broth), fresh lobster and crab, or Japanese *wagyu* beef. Guests can take in a full day of spa pampering, soak in the healing waters, and indulge in a formal *kaiseki* dinner in the privacy of their own traditional tatami room or in one of the select rooms that accommodate parties of different sizes. The overnight stay includes Western or Japanese breakfast the next morning.

CRITICS' TIPS

There is only one menu served each month so if you are staying multiple nights, request a change in the courses to experience a wider range of dishes or opt for a more simple meal such as sukiyaki *or* shabu-shabu.

Be prepared to sit on the floor for meals while staying here.

1300 GÔRA, HAKONE-MACHI, ASHIGARASHIMO-GUN, KANAGAWA 250-0408
+81 460 82 3331
WWW.GORAKADAN.COM/KADAN

HOT POT OF LONGTOOTH GROUPER WITH HOMEMADE FRIED TOFU

GION SASAKI

[JAPANESE KAISEKI] Seats are often booked a year in advance at this venerable Kyoto institution, which has established itself as one of the top destinations for unparalleled *kaiseki* dishes as elaborate in presentation as they are bold in flavor. Chef Hiroshi Sasaki presides over the counter-style seating, ensuring an intimate, exclusive audience for his traditional fare. Local food lovers know to order the Rausu sea urchin and sweet white shrimp, which is artfully plated between blanched *zuiki* (sweet potato stem) enfolded in a gelée of tomato water. Equally revered is the clay-pot-cooked rice crowned with grilled *sanma* (Pacific saury fish) plucked fresh from the nearby waters of Hokkaido and garnished with grated daikon and picked *mibuna* (leafy green vegetable). Dishes such as the beloved sashimi platter display Sasaki's penchant for structured, purposeful dishes. Order it and you might receive tender raw octopus, charred pike eel, toothsome *kuruma* prawn, and buttery *toro* (fatty tuna) sushi plated for two and accompanied by a measured mound of fresh wasabi. Increasing the attraction, this top-quality experience in *kaiseki* cuisine comes at less than half the price of those offered at larger Kyoto establishments.

CRITICS' TIPS

This is one of Kyoto's most difficult reservations to secure, so call well ahead of time.

The meal starts for all diners at 6:30 p.m. sharp and everyone needs be seated before the chef gets started, so be on time!

Bring plenty of yen; this is a cash-only establishment.

566-27 KOMATSU-CHO, YAMATOOJI HIGASHI
HAIRU, YASAKA-DORI, HIGASHIYAMA-KU,
KYOTO 605-0811
+81 75 551 5000
WWW.GIONSASAKI.COM

RED SNAPPER SASHIMI

HAMASAKU

[JAPANESE] Hamasaku has been impressing visitors, dignitaries, and celebrities from Charlie Chaplin to Prince Charles for more than 80 years with its exemplary rendition of classical Kyoto-style cuisine. Equal parts *kaseiki* (multicourse dinner), *kappo* (Japanese counter fine dining), café, and cooking school, the third-generation family-run restaurant set in a traditional two-story teahouse in Kyoto's Higashiyama-ku area continues to attract food lovers with its diverse selection of dining options. For the ambitious guest, the two prime choices are the first-floor Western-style dining room serving formal *omakase* dinners or the first-floor wood counter fashioned out of a 250-year-old cypress slab. At the counter, the newest generation, represented by Chef Hiroyuki Morikawa, presents updated Gion cuisine featuring seasonal specialties, such as highly lauded sea bream sashimi and crispy whole-fried turbot seasoned with bouillon. Completing the culinary trifecta is the Salon de Café Anti Dilettante, which is a "Western style" café serving coffee, house-made pastries, and an affordable à la carte lunch menu. Together, they create a mixture of culture and experience that cannot be had anywhere else.

CRITICS' TIPS

If you're part of a larger group, request to sit in the upstairs private dining room, which accommodates up to 10 people.

If you're here at night, visit the Salon de Café Anti Dilettante, which takes on more of a bar atmosphere, offering a wide selection of beer and spirits and, on occasion, live piano music.

Consider taking a cooking class, which is taught on site by the chef.

498 SHIMOKAWARA-MACHI, YASAKA TORIIMAE-KUDARU, GION, HIGASHIYAMA-KU, KYOTO 605-0825
+81 75 561 0330
WWW.HAMASAKU.COM

ROAST DUCK WITH JAPANESE *NITSUKE* SAUCE

KAPPO MASUDA

[JAPANESE KAPPO] Diners lucky enough to secure one of the seven counter seats or four tatami rooms at this Kyoto landmark will be mesmerized by Chef-Owner Takashi Masuda's masterful *Kyo-ryōri* cuisine—Kyoto-style food known for its distinct sophistication, visual beauty, and subtlety of taste. Often referred to as the pinnacle of Japanese cuisine, the *kaiseki*-style fare served here celebrates fresh seafood and Japanese beef, ceremoniously prepared and presented in 10 to 12 courses by Masuda-san and his son, Satoshi Masuda. Chef Masuda's wife presents perfect pairings of sake, wine, beer, and tea to accompany the seasonal dishes. The *omakase* (chef's choice) menu, typical of most Kyoto *kappo* (counter-seating) restaurants, allows Masuda-san's mastery to truly shine. Order it and expect refined presentations of fresh *hamo* (pike eel) sushi, giant grilled snow crab from the Sea of Japan, abalone sashimi, and the finest quality seared Japanese beef with matsutake mushrooms—all gorgeously presented on colorful ceramic vessels thoughtfully selected to complement the season and dish. Fitting for a culinary master with *kokoro*, or "heart," as one of our critics describes, Masuda ensures this family-run experience is faultless—and endearing—from start to finish.

CRITICS' TIPS

Take note: to secure a reservation, you probably need an invitation from a Kyoto native who is known to the chef.

Definitely order Chef Masuda's secret drink: a block of pure ice shaped to fit a tumbler perfectly, swirled, and finished with a great single malt scotch or whiskey, or his selection of local, unusual sake.

Don't leave without perusing the photograph wall of famous patrons, including geisha performers, artists, and Japanese celebrities.

682 ISHIFUDOUNO-CHO, GOKO-MACHI NISHI-IRU,
MATSUBARA-DORI, SIMOGYOU-KU, KYOTO-SHI,
KYOTO 600-8047
+81 75 361 1508

SOFT ROE AND TOFU MILK PASTE IN A *YUZU* CITRUS "STOVE" WITH PONZU SAUCE

KIKUNOI HONTEN

[JAPANESE KAISEKI] Yoshihiro Murata—one of Kyoto's most famous chefs, an undisputed master of *kaiseki* cuisine, and the third-generation chef-owner of renowned Kikunoi Honten—offers an authentic taste of Kyoto. Within the traditional Japanese *ryōtei* (luxurious Japanese restaurant), Chef Murata expertly balances tradition and innovation, anchoring his *kaiseki* dishes in their sixteenth-century culinary origins while evolving them with the seasons and latest cooking trends. Upon arrival, guests are escorted to their own private dining room, where they begin a journey through perhaps 14 courses, each more expertly crafted than the last. Each meal begins with a *sakizuke*, or appetizer, often accompanied by *shincha* tea or ceremonial sake. Menus are seasonal and may include a grilled course of salt-crusted *ayu* (sweetfish) nestled on a bed of bamboo leaves, or sashimi garnished with spicy *sansho* Japanese pepper flowers or chrysanthemum petals. Décor exhibits a sense of seasonality with revolving artwork and floral arrangements. However, no matter what time of year, you'll be treated to an exploration of food and Japanese history that illustrates why Kikunoi and Chef Murata remain pillars of the Kyoto dining scene.

CRITICS' TIPS

Try to visit in the spring or fall when the colors and food of Kyoto are especially fantastic.

Book very far in advance and simultaneously let them know if there is anything your party won't eat; since the meal is omakase, *or chef's choice, it's not easy for the chef to accommodate requests on the spot.*

If you come during winter, don't miss the grilled snow crab. It is the best you'll ever experience.

459 SHIMOKAWARA-CHO, YASAKATORIIMAE-SAGARU,
SHIMOKAWARA-DORI, HIGASHIYAMA-KU,
KYOTO-SHI, KYOTO 605-0825
+81 75 561 0015
WWW.KIKUNOI.JP

STEAMED CHERRY BLOSSOM *MOCHI* CAKE OF TILEFISH AND LILY ROOT

KINMATA

[JAPANESE KAISEKI] Located on the outskirts of the bustling Kawaramachi and Shinkyogoku districts and run by fifth-generation owner and head chef Haruji Ukai, one of Kyoto's most well-preserved *ryokans* (traditional Japanese inns) is also home to some of the region's most inventive *kaiseki* fare. The multicourse menu is strongly influenced by the traditional and contemporary and the freshest ingredients available at the neighboring Nishiki market. Still, a stringent sense of history and authenticity is evident in everything from the surroundings to the museum-quality ceramics (some of which are century-old family heirlooms) on which the food is served. Seated in the main dining room—overnight guests may also choose to eat in the privacy of their tatami rooms—your multicourse meal is sure to be full of intricately prepared surprises, such as a subtly flavored, bracken-fern-garnished tilefish and lily root dumpling in a delicate clear broth (pictured at left) or fresh-water eel with daikon radish on a sunshine-yellow sesame custard. With faultless service, lush gardens, and welcoming atmosphere, there may be no better way to savor the distinctly elegant flavors of Kyoto.

CRITICS' TIPS

For the full experience, book a tatami room facing the ryokan's garden in the back and enjoy the food in your room.

Consider dining here even if you are staying elsewhere; this is one of the only Kyoto ryokans that offers a kaiseki meal without an overnight stay.

To truly experience the Japanese art of tea, order the thin- or thick-powdered matcha tea after lunch or dinner.

SHIJO-AGARU GOKOMACHI, NAKAGYO-KU,
KYOTO-SHI, KYOTO 604-8044
+81 75 221 1039
WWW.KINMATA.COM

RED SNAPPER, SQUID, AND TUNA SASHIMI

KITCHO ARASHIYAMA

[JAPANESE KAISEKI] Set against a backdrop of the Arashiyama Mountain and the Ōi River, Kitcho Arashiyama is so captivating that it commands attention despite its breathtaking surroundings. Not only a restaurant but a museum of Japanese culture, its heritage-inspired food, kimono-clad servers, individual garden-view tatami rooms, and antique serving dishes underscore Chef Kunio Tokuoka's commitment to offering the best of traditional luxury fine dining. With complete privacy, there are no distractions from Chef Tokuoka's *kaiseki*-style meal, which invariably showcases his revolutionary brand of Kyoto cuisine. Fresh, creative, sometimes international, and always infusing the traditional with contemporary influences, menus are decidedly seasonal, infused with the bounty of the fertile region and showcasing color and contrast in the Japanese tradition. Intricately prepared and plated, the day's offerings might include sea bream, tuna sashimi, and matsutake mushrooms in summer, or perhaps a consommé in autumn. One of the most noteworthy dishes "white rice" defies seasonality and expectation. This heavenly, hand-selected blend of grains is combined with soy sauce and bonito to conjure what one of our critics describes as "the essence of Japanese cuisine."

CRITICS' TIPS

If possible, come for lunch rather than for dinner to enjoy the landscape and garden view in the daylight.

If you are comfortable eating raw egg, try the secret "rice with raw egg" dish. It's very memorable.

Visit during February's annual Setsubun bean-scattering festival, which is held each year the day before spring.

58 SUSUKINOBABA-CHO, SAGA TENRYUJI, UKYO-KU,
KYOTO-SHI, KYOTO 616-8385
+81 75 881 1101
WWW.KITCHO.COM/KYOTO/SHOPLIST_EN/
ARASHIYAMA/INDEX.HTML

GRILLED WILD *AYU* (SWEETFISH)

KODAIJI WAKUDEN

[JAPANESE] In the shadow of the seventeenth-century Kodaiji temple, Wakuden offers its own taste of Japanese history. From the building's streamlined traditional décor and its counter seating to the handmade ceramics that vary with the seasons and the lovingly prepared local cuisine, Wakuden evokes both a simpler time and an authentic Japanese experience. Natural light suffuses the dining room with a delicate glow, and seats at the long counter offer spectacular views of Kyoto's Gion neighborhood. Seats in the coveted tatami-mat room provide views of a different kind: of your food, made from seasonal ingredients, being cooked on an *irori*, a traditional sunken hearth. In winter months, the meal might be grilled winter crab, at its best in Japan between December and February. Red snapper and tuna also star in colder months, though they might appear as a pristine sashimi. Aotakeshu, Wakuden's own sake, provides a perfect accompaniment. The combination of flawless service and exquisite food create an experience that seems almost more like art than dining.

CRITICS' TIPS

Wakuden does not take reservations, so plan accordingly.

Try to come during winter; it's a special time to visit.

It is rare to be seated in the room with the irori *fireplace, but hope for it. It's the best room in the house.*

512 WASHIO-CHO, KODAIJI KITAMONN-MAE, HIGASHIYAMA-KU, KYOTO-SHI, KYOTO 605-0072
+81 75 533 3100
WWW.WAKUDEN.JP/RYOTEI/
KODAIJI/INDEX_E.HTML

MARINATED MACKEREL SUSHI

MIYAMASOU

[JAPANESE KAISEKI] Nestled up on forested Mount Miyama, about an hour-long car ride from central Kyoto, Miyamasou offers travelers the quintessential classical Japanese dining experience. The restaurant itself is located in a classic *ryokan*, a traditional country inn comprising low-slung, wooden temple-like buildings where overnight guests can soak up the serene surroundings. Diners at the restaurant will undoubtedly do the same. Each morning, Chef Hisato Nakahigashi forages the neighboring fields, forests, and rivers to collect the ingredients for his nightly *kaiseki* dinners prepared in the *tsumikusa-ryōri* (young herb cuisine) style of cooking. Inside the dining room, surrounded on all sides by *shoji* sliding glass doors overlooking the idyllic setting, guests sit on cushions around a rectangular-shaped chestnut counter. In its center the chef works his magic, meticulously preparing a series of little dishes, such as carp sashimi, salt-baked bamboo shoots, and grilled fresh shrimp, then artfully arranging them on simple lacquerware designed to highlight the pristine ingredients. If you're spending the night or have a designated driver, allow the kimono-clad waitresses to pair each course with sake.

CRITICS' TIPS

The journey to the restaurant is one hour by car and nearly two hours each way via subway or shuttle bus, so consider booking one of the four guest rooms at least a week in advance and spend the night.

Dress for comfort and agility: Seating consists of cushioned wood benches around sunken tables or on woven tatami mats on the floor.

If you can't make it to this mountaintop retreat, try visiting Oku, the chef's casual café in Kyoto's Gion district, where he offers sampler plates of Miyamasou cuisine.

375 DAIHIZAN, HANASEHARACHI-CHO, SAKYO-KU, KYOTO-SHI, KYOTO 601-1102
+81 75 746 0231
MIYAMASOU.JP/HTML_EN/INDEX.HTML

SESAME TOFU AND WHITE MISO SOUP WITH RICE

MIZAI

[JAPANESE KAISEKI] Located in an old teahouse in the center of Kyoto's Maruyama Park and requiring reservations of six months to a year in advance, Mizai is hailed as one of the best practitioners of tea-ceremony-type *kaiseki* cuisine in Japan. The short walk through the park to the restaurant, escorted by an apprentice holding lanterns to guide the way, is the first hint of the drama to follow. Upon reaching the porch, guests are invited to sip tea before taking their seats at the lacquered 14-seat counter. This is where the theater truly begins as Chef Hitoshi Ishihara, who trained at Kyoto's highly regarded Arashiyama Kitcho, displays his showmanship, presenting a parade of sophisticated dishes on beautifully handcrafted pottery bowls and plates designed to express the spirit of the season. The meal begins traditionally with tea service and a bowl of rice served with seasonal pickles, a deceptive simply dish that reveals just how delicious perfectly prepared rice can be. Other favorites are sashimi served with freshly grated wasabi and cubes of soy sauce gelée and luxuriously marbled *wagyu* beef. An *ichiban*-arrangement of fruits suspended in a champagne jelly marks the closing act of this piece of dining theater.

CRITICS' TIPS

All guests are asked to arrive at 6 p.m. Don't be late because everyone is seated at the same time and the meal will not be served until everyone is present.

Prepare to put away your camera; the chef doesn't allow photographs to be taken in the dining room.

The restaurant is cash only so bring plenty of yen, particularly if you avail yourself of the restaurant's premier beer and sake collection.

INSIDE MARUYAMA PARK
613 MARUYAMA-CHO HIGASHI-IRU, YASAKATORIIMAE
HIGASHIYAMA-KU, KYOTO 605-0071
+81 75 551 3310
WWW.MIZAI.JP

ASSORTED NEW YEAR APPETIZERS

SAKURADA

[JAPANESE KAISEKI] Despite its hidden location down a pedestrian back alley in an unmarked house, Sakurada is one of the Karasuma district's most well-known restaurants. Its owner, Chef Isuzu Sakurada, hails from the venerable *ryōtei*-style Shofukuro restaurant where he honed the craft of tea-ceremony-style *kaiseki,* a procession of courses inspired by and meant to evoke the seasons. At Sakurada, traditional *kaiseki* style is honored in an understated dining room with little more than a few dark wood tables, counter seats, shoji screens, and one tatami room that seats up to eight guests. But the remarkable little plates of Japanese haute cuisine presented in an array of one-of-a-kind ceramic bowls, plates, trays, and lacquer boxes make a meal here a feast for both the eyes and the palate. Signature dishes come and go; with spring may arrive fresh bamboo shoots simmered in broth, and during winter a sushi bento box. But a perennial favorite is the *hassun,* an elaborately composed seafood- and vegetable-based first course that sets the season's theme. The meal culminates majestically with a mélange of fruit desserts and cups of tea ferried out by quietly doting kimono-clad waitresses.

CRITICS' TIPS

Given its tiny size, dinner reservations are hard to come by, so instead consider the more easily accessed set-lunch menu, which costs about half the price of dinner.

Bring plenty of yen; the restaurant accepts cash only.

While seeking out this clandestine spot, look for the green and white split curtains for the entrance.

634-2 NIOITENJIN-CHO, HITOSUJI-SAGARU,
BUKKOJI HIGASHI-IRU, KARASUMA, SIMOGYO-KU,
KYOTO-SHI, KYOTO 600-8184
+81 75 371 2552

AN ASSORTED KYOTO VEGETABLES APPETIZER

SHUHAKU

[JAPANESE] Shuhaku may be "small and simple," one of our critics says, "yet it's one of Kyoto's top Japanese restaurants." This intimate counter-seating-only establishment is owned and operated by Chef Nobuhisa Yoshida, who spent his early years in the kitchens of French restaurants in Kyoto. As a result, his enchanting evolution of traditional Kyoto-style fare is a wholly new and impressive version of Japanese cuisine that integrates French technique. As with the best of both cuisines, dishes are seasonal, highlighting the freshest local ingredients. In the summer, menus might include a seasonal hot vegetable "salad"—a striking presentation of more than 20 different types of Kyoto vegetables. Ayu (sweetfish) begins appearing on the menu in June, when the fish grows to ample size, as an artful sushi presentation that literally illustrates the passage of time in Kyoto cuisine. Chef Yoshida embellishes the experience with his personal Franco-centric wine collection, featuring great white and red Burgundies with local sakes and select beers, resulting in a unique and highly personal experience of French-Kyoto fare that you won't find anywhere else.

CRITICS' TIPS

Don't try to come on the days the restaurant is closed—Monday and the third Sunday of every month.

Try the dashi (broth). The chef perfectly harmonizes Japanese and French influences by combining traditional Japanese soup stock with French ingredients. It's very unique.

Take advantage of the wine list. Yoshida began collecting French wines while studying regional cuisine in France, and he offers wonderful selections at very reasonable prices.

392 KANEZONO-CHO, YASAKATOUNOMAE-AGARU,
SHIMOGAWARA-DORI, HIGASHIYAMA-KU,
KYOTO-SHI, KYOTO 605-0828
+81 75 551 2711

"PLANET EARTH"

HAJIME

[MODERN FRENCH] Despite its incognito location on a backstreet in Osaka, this supremely innovative modern French restaurant named after the young chef-owner Hajime Yoneda hardly flies under the radar. The restaurant opened in 2008 and, with its understated gray slate floors, white walls, and well-spaced tables, it quickly shot to fame as one of the city's finest for its spontaneous high-end tasting menus that marry the creativity of molecular gastronomy, classical techniques of French cooking, and Japanese cultural devotion to the natural world. Chef Yoneda trained at the Hokkaido outpost of French chef Michel Bras before setting out on his own, and the influence is evidenced by the *amuse-bouche* that starts the meal and the avant-garde desserts, such as frozen popcorn, that end it. In between are myriad surprises, which might include his signature dish, "The Mineral," a cornucopia of 66 exquisite seasonal vegetables, grains, and herbs artfully arranged around a pool of shellfish foam. Other revelations include foie gras served "au naturel"—a dish one of our critics deems "one of the best foie gras dishes in the world." Service is attentive from beginning to end, when the chef is known to personally bid guests adieu on their way out the door.

CRITICS' TIPS

If you're having trouble getting a reservation by phone, try booking through the website.

Consider coming for a midday meal when the set-lunch menu costs half the price of dinner.

Engage the restaurant's sommelier, who will happily provide wine pairings for each course, if desired.

1-9-11-1F, EDOBORI, NISHI-KU
OSAKA-SHI, OSAKA 550-0002
+81 6 6447 6688
WWW.HAJIME-ARTISTES.COM

BUTTER-SAUTÉED WILD ABALONE AND ASPARAGAS WITH
EGG YOLK–MAYONNAISE SAUCE

KIGAWA ASAI

[JAPANESE] When confronted with the simply written à la carte menu posted on the kitchen wall at Kigawa Asai, it's easy to feel overwhelmed. With more than 100 dishes listed—only in Japanese—it might seem simpler to order *omakase*, or chef's choice. Either way, the rewards are the same. Few restaurants of this caliber offer such a vast array of dishes to explore, especially à la carte. Chef Koreto Kubo clearly tries to evoke a strong sense of Osaka, from the cuisine highlighting local, seasonal ingredients to the classic décor. Despite its vastness, Kubo's menu changes daily, based on the freshest, highest-quality ingredients available at the moment. The dishes also combine Eastern and Western influences to great effect, especially in the restaurant's trademark abalone; though Japanese in nature, the delicate mollusk is accompanied by asparagus and a mayonnaise and butter sauce. You'll also find a classic beef fillet. Steamed and broiled eel from Shiga's Lake Biwa is another standout. Whether you sit at the gleaming wood counter, at one of the simple elegant tables, or in a traditional tatami room, Kigawa Asai offers an experience that no other Osaka restaurant can match.

CRITICS' TIPS

You can order a bento box lunch to go, with three unique choices: Japanese style, Western style, or seasonal rice.

Conclude your meal with the plum porridge made with yoshino-kudzu (the starchy root of an eastern Asian vine).

ROYAL NAKAYA 1F
1-6-19 HIGASHI-SHINSAIBASHI, CHUO-KU, OSAKA 542-0083
+81 6 6243 7100
WWW2.OCN.NE.JP/~K-ASAI

A SEASONAL FALL APPETIZER

KOKIN AOYAGI

[JAPANESE] Perched above the Naruto Strait in Setonaikai National Park near Tokushima, Kokin Aoyagi doesn't simply offer stunning views of the surrounding gardens, sea, and islands; it's the very expression of the region. A favorite of many critics and the training grounds for myriad now-famous Japanese chefs, it's the flagship of one of Japan's most celebrated chefs, Hirohisa Koyama, who took it over from his grandfather. The setting is unapologetically traditional with wood beams, shoji screens, sunken tatami seating, and a chef's counter, but Koyama has breathed new life into the landmark space with his utterly contemporary take on his country's cuisine. In true *kaiseki* tradition, there is no set menu, just an ever-changing procession of almost-too-pretty-to-eat compositions inspired by the seasons and local larder. Not surprising, the menu leans heavily toward ultrafresh seafood with the likes of marinated octopus and fried conger eel. Certainly don't miss the chef's signature *Tai no tantan*, featuring the iconic red snapper found in the strait's strong currents served over perfectly seasoned sushi rice. This deceptively simple dish exemplifies Koyama's meticulous sourcing, virtuoso knife skills, and cooking expertise.

CRITICS' TIPS

The rustic wooden ranch house with unobstructed sea views is a serene setting, but for an especially traditional dining experience, request one of the private tatami rooms.

The red snapper from Japan's Naruto area is a must-try, so don't even think of passing it up.

1-1 AZA-NAKAYAMA, OSHIMADA, SETO-CHO, NARUTO-SHI, TOKUSHIMA 771-0367
+81 88 688 1155
WWW.KOKIN-AOYAGI.JP

THE UNITED STATES

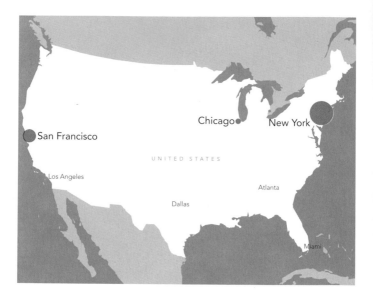

NEW YORK AREA

MIDWEST

SAN FRANCISCO BAY AREA

BAKED WILD STRIPED BASS, BRAISED DAIKON, AND *PIQUILLO* PEPPERS WITH ADOBO SAUCE

LE BERNARDIN

[FRENCH SEAFOOD] More than 25 years after brother-sister culinary duo Gilbert and Maguy Le Coze opened Le Bernardin, the French seafood mainstay continues to hold its four-star status longer than any other New York establishment. The youngest four-star chef in the city when he became executive chef in 1994, Co-Owner Eric Ripert has an encyclopedic knowledge of classical French culinary technique, which he employs to create flawlessly and faultlessly creative dishes that perpetuate Le Bernardin's house mantra, "The fish is the star of the plate." His seasonal fixed-price menu—with options ranging from "Almost Raw" to "Barely Touched" to "Lightly Cooked"—takes an increasingly minimalistic approach to delivering simple, yet highly sophisticated seafood that's heavily influenced by global flavors. Consequently, garnishes of "almond-pistachio-barberry" golden basmati and brown-butter tamarind vinaigrette make the natural flavor of a perfectly sautéed Dover sole even more eloquent. The menu is paired with the notoriously impeccable service of exceptional maître d' Ben Chekroun and award-winning sommelier Aldo Sohm and his 900 wines. Add to that a recently redesigned interior and Le Bernardin remains one of the biggest fish in a large, highly competitive pond.

CRITICS' TIPS

If you prefer to dine à la carte, secure a seat in the lounge.

If sea urchin pasta is offered, don't pass it up, and always inquire about the off-menu catch of the day.

Request the pounded tuna, which features thin layers of the delicate fish and foie gras on a toasted baguette—it's a dance of flavors and a tangle of textures.

155 WEST 51ST STREET
NEW YORK, NY 10019
212.554.1515
WWW.LE-BERNARDIN.COM

DRY-AGED *POULET ROUGE* (CHICKEN), PORCINI MUSHROOMS, AND
KOHLRABI BROTH

BLANCA

[ITALIAN] Tucked in the back of popular Brooklyn pizzeria Roberta's, Chef Carlo Mirarchi has created a unique and sought-after dining experience with Blanca, his 12-seat "tasting room" that's open solely for dinner Wednesday through Saturday. Blanca is adorned with a decorative bluefin-tuna head, a vintage turntable, and one single L-shaped counter, which affords a front-row view of Mirarchi and team at work in the sparkling stainless-steel kitchen. Each night's take-it-or-leave-it menu, which is never the same, features more than 20 unconventional, often exhilarating preparations that meld flavors and textures in unexpected ways. Though Mirarchi's food is influenced by Italian cuisine, his reinterpretations catapult the familiar into wholly new culinary territory. Raw glass shrimp might arrive adorned with celery flower, celery juice, and poppy seeds, while classic beef carpaccio is updated with duck-egg yolk. Only the requisite and consistently exceptional pasta course, such as *agnolotti* filled with "melting" pine-nut sauce, pointedly underscores the Italian sentiment. Desserts, perhaps watermelon-radish gelato with cubes of pressed watermelon and sour watermelon gummies, are as inventive as the preceding courses.

CRITICS' TIPS

With few seats, the restaurant books well in advance and reserves only one month out. For the best shot at securing a seat, call the first day of the month.

Try the sake, beer, and wine pairings with the food. They're worthy enhancements.

261 MOORE STREET
BROOKLYN, NY 11206
347.799.2807
WWW.BLANCANYC.COM

PORCHETTA WITH ARTICHOKE, CHANTERELLES, DAYLILIES, KALE, "SAMANTHA" CABBAGE, AND "SAUCE CHARCUTERIE"

BLUE HILL AT STONE BARNS

[SEASONAL AMERICAN] Aptly located in New York's bucolic Hudson Valley, Blue Hill at Stone Barns is more than a restaurant; it's a dream about sustainability, a total farm-to-table vision realized by brothers Dan and David Barber long before the concept became trendy. Chef Dan Barber offers diners a choice of five-, eight-, or twelve-course "farmer's feasts," each of which reflects the day's harvest. Before they eat, diners are encouraged to go out into the fields, visit the animals, and understand where the food is coming from. It doesn't take long to realize the Barbers don't just want to feed you—they want to enlighten you. Adding to the pastoral enchantment, the dining area is an old dairy barn with high beams and soaring windows that offer incomparable views of the surrounding countryside. Not surprising, vegetables are outstanding here, as is the pork. Fresh produce even finds its way into libations, such as their proprietary liqueurs, which might include lemon verdana or geranium and oats. If infused cocktails don't entice you, enlist the expertise of wine director and Jean-Georges–alum Charles Puglia to help navigate the 40-page, 1,000-plus-label list, which spans from California to Burgundy and beyond.

CRITICS' TIPS

Don't let the out-of-town location deter you. From Manhattan you can reach the restaurant easily via a 35-minute express train and 10-minute cab ride.

Visit during the fall when the harvest is at its best, or in the summer when the extended warm evening light spills over the surrounding fields.

Do take a moment to explore the grounds, which are stunning as well as educational.

630 BEDFORD ROAD
POCANTICO HILLS, NY 10591
914.366.9600
WWW.BLUEHILLFARM.COM/FOOD/
BLUE-HILL-STONE-BARNS

CHERRYWOOD-SMOKED DUCK BREAST OVER DASHI-SOFTENED
BUCKWHEAT AND KABOCHA SQUASH

BRUSHSTROKE

[JAPANESE] A collaboration between New York chef and restaurant mogul David Bouley and Yoshiki Tsuji, the president of Japan's revered Osaka-based Tsuji Culinary Institute, Brushstroke emphasizes *kaiseki* cuisine, or Japanese small-plate multicourse meals, artfully crafted from seasonal ingredients. Within this Tribeca gem decorated in the spartan style of a Shinto shrine, Head Chef Isao Yamada, a master of the traditional cooking style, offers fixed-price menus as well as an *omakase* (chef's choice) menu, the latter of which he tailors to the diner's individual palate. All served on carefully chosen dishes to enhance the experience, the food wows, perhaps with a lush *chawan mushi* steamed egg custard with velvety crab and black truffle, expertly prepared and sliced *wagyu* beef, or delicate lobster dumplings. At the tiny sushi bar, sushi master Eiji Ichimura quietly turns out some of the most stunning sushi in New York. Cocktails made with seasonal fruits, vegetables, and Japanese herbs make stellar accompaniments, while desserts, such as soy-milk *panna cotta* with *matcha* sauce, surprise and delight. With rice-paper window coverings and bare honey-colored wood, the room matches the food with its airy, modern Zen feel.

CRITICS' TIPS

Sit at the counter facing the open kitchen so you can watch the display of kitchen artistry.

Don't miss the artisanal sakes and infusions.

Take time to admire the collage wall; look carefully and you'll see small dioramas of daily life in Japan.

30 HUDSON STREET
NEW YORK, NY 10013
212.791.3771
WWW.DAVIDBOULEY.COM/
BRUSHSTROKE-MAIN

HOW TO SECURE
THE MOST COVETED
RESERVATIONS

Not that long ago it took little more than a timely phone call to reserve a table at a great restaurant. Now that dining has become a top form of entertainment, access to some of the world's most coveted spots has become as challenging as securing front-row seats to a Broadway opening.

Today it's commonplace for diners to mark their calendars months in advance and call a restaurant from multiple phone lines at the magic moment reservations open—and even then success is far from assured. Consider The French Laundry (p. 185). Nearly two decades ago, it trained diners to call diligently and exactly two months in advance, and it's still one of the nation's hardest reservations to secure. The odds aren't any better at Denmark's Noma (p. 201), which takes reservations three months out and gets an average of more than 20,000 requests for any given month. Chicago's Alinea (p. 177), which sells "tickets" for its tasting menu, alerts diners of openings on its Facebook page. Like arena concert tickets, seats often come available—with a steep surcharge—on Craigslist's online classifieds.

That doesn't mean you'll never sit at one of these coveted tables. Next time you want to book one of the restaurants in this guide, try these tactics:

Call—a lot. Press redial repeatedly and often to get through to a restaurant flooded with reservations requests. Perseverance often pays off—especially if you are flexible on your desired date. You might be able to secure a table through a recent cancellation.

Leverage online reservations. Even the most exclusive restaurants now use online reservations systems. Learn a restaurant's reservations policies in advance and make sure you're online and requesting a table at the appropriate time. You'll have as good a chance as anyone in securing a seat.

Email. Not all restaurants respond to email, but many do their best to keep up with correspondence. A written request, especially for overseas reservations, can be extremely helpful. We've heard myriad tales of people who wrote very personal emails stating who they were, when and why they wanted to come, and how they could be contacted in case a table came available and consequently got to enjoy the meal of a lifetime.

Use your connections. If you're a foodie, you probably know someone who knows someone with a connection to your desired restaurant, perhaps a maître d' or another staff member. Have them call on your behalf. In the restaurant reservations game, who you know truly can make the difference.

Turn to the concierge. You can have great luck securing reservations if you seek help from your hotel's or credit card company's concierge. Restaurants often save a table or two for important unexpected guests, and they also receive last minute cancellations. The business of a concierge is to be well connected, and he or she can make miracles happen.

Get a local to correspond on your behalf. If you're intending to dine abroad in an area where you don't speak the language, recruit someone locally to speak on your behalf. A native speaker ensures no miscommunications are made, and he or she might make the difference in getting a table at all. This is especially true in Japan, where restaurants often consider locals their top priority as well as the most reliable diners, since cultural notions of honor and respect ensure guests won't no-show or cancel at the last minute.

Chase cancellations. Even the best, most exclusive destination restaurants have last-minute cancellations. On the day you want to dine, call or go by the restaurant in person. Linger in the restaurant's vicinity and you have a solid chance of getting into the dining room—especially at out-of-the way locations on rainy days.

SEARED SCALLOP, MOREL, WHITE ASPARAGUS, GREEN ALMONDS, AND SHELLFISH FOAM

CHEF'S TABLE AT BROOKLYN FARE

[MODERN] At this diminutive Brooklyn eatery, Chef César Ramírez bans cell phones, smartphones, and even note-taking. Your focus, like his, must be entirely on the food. But you won't be sorry. The only concern is getting one of the 18 seats at the gleaming stainless-steel counter, as reservations aren't easy to come by. Beneath rows of lustrous copper pots, Ramírez and his crew create an ever-changing tasting menu of Japanese cuisine with French influences from the freshest ingredients available. Seafood reigns, and Ramírez's blowfish—served legally, when available—is a work of art. Octopus simmered in dashi comes with heart of palm and a tiny dot of searing sansho pepper, an exquisite combination of zest and heat. Other standouts include langoustine tempura enhanced with Iranian saffron, salmon with trout eggs, and anything caviar. Ramírez dispenses advice for each of his petite dishes, from the best utensil to use to the optimum number of bites it should take. The Eurocentric wine list is, like the menu, stellar.

CRITICS' TIPS

The restaurant takes reservations six weeks in advance, only by phone, and only for parties of two or four. Call Monday morning for the best chance of securing a table.

Don't be late for your reservation. With very limited seating, food service starts promptly for each sitting.

Don't hesitate to ask for help with the surprisingly extensive wine list.

200 SCHERMERHORN STREET
BROOKLYN, NY 11201
718.243.0050
WWW.BROOKLYNFARE.COM/
PAGES/CHEFS-TABLE

MILK-FED VEAL TENDERLOIN WITH OREGON MORELS,
CHEEKS WITH FAVA BEAN COULIS, AND CRISPY SWEETBREADS
WITH TARRAGON PASTA

DANIEL

[FRENCH] Within the formal silvery gray and chocolate brown Adam D. Tihany–designed dining room, Chef-Owner Daniel Boulud and Executive Chef Jean François Bruel present perfectly prepared modern French food in an absolutely classic manner. For this reason many of our critics agree Daniel is perhaps New York's most reliable restaurant for great food and service. Dishes often link to Boulud's time in the kitchen of Roger Vergé in Mougins, France, and to his Lyonnais heritage. Complex presentations feature many items bolstering the star of the plate, be it a trio of Coho salmon, a mackerel tasting, or a duo of Elysian Field lamb chops with roasted fennel and arugula salad, fig-balsamic-glazed confit ribs, and Tarbais bean purée. Desserts are also aggressively accessorized, with two pages of choices, including one just for chocolate desserts. Service merges smart, proper French style with welcoming warmth, and extends to a spectacular wine list with an ambitious selection, all under $100. Perfecting the experience is a sweet finale; every meal ends with a chorus of small sweets, cookies, chocolates, and Boulud's signature madeleines still warm from the oven and nestled in a napkin cozy.

CRITICS' TIPS

For a prime location, request the corner banquette in the central area down two steps—or a balcony table for more privacy.

Come during the game season for the house's homage to classics, such as canard au sang *or farm venison with cocoa bean shavings and sauce* Grand Veneur.

Park Avenue regulars and bargain hunters know that you can order à la carte in the lounge.

60 EAST 65TH STREET
NEW YORK, NY 10065
212.288.0033
WWW.DANIELNYC.COM

CRUDO OF MAINE DIVER SCALLOP WITH GRAPEFRUIT, KUMQUAT, JALAPEÑO, AND PANSIES

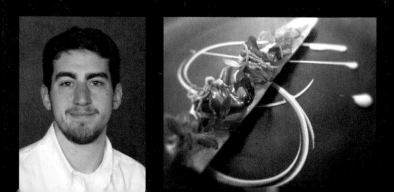

DEGUSTATION

🚜   ✉

[SPANISH] One of the more diminutive jewels in restaurateur Jack Lamb's East Village empire, this 19-seat spot evokes the tapas bars of Spain. However, Chef Nicholas Licata's style is more international: It's Spanish with touches of French, Japanese, and even modernist cuisine. All the seats around the U-shape blonde-wood bar face a gleaming stainless-steel kitchen, providing perfect vantage points from which to watch the culinary transformations happen. In Licata's nimble hands, classic Spanish tortilla becomes something else entirely: airy poached quail egg and shallot confit folded into potato slices. Fried anchovies, a tapas staple, are triumphantly paired with oatmeal risotto and garlic aioli. Flavors are bigger and bolder than the delicate presentations would suggest, even in the case of dessert, which might include blowtorched strawberries or caramelized *torija*, Licata's gooey iteration of bread pudding. A tasting menu is offered, and myriad enticing options and small portions make sampling a variety of offerings an attractive proposition. Like everything else about Degustation, the wine list is small. But what it lacks in quantity, it more than makes up for in quality and diversity.

CRITICS' TIPS

Don't book a table if you're looking for a romantic evening. A meal here is entirely about the making and enjoyment of food.

Start the meal with a glass of rosé cava, then explore one of the list's stellar Spanish white or red wines.

239 EAST 5TH STREET
NEW YORK, NY 10003
212.979.1012

YELLOWFIN TUNA RIBBONS WITH AVOCADO, SPICY RADISH, AND GINGER MARINADE

JEAN-GEORGES

[FRENCH] Despite his far-flung restaurant empire, French chef Jean-Georges Vongerichten continues to turn out exciting food in his flagship restaurant, which is one of New York's most appealing dining rooms. The airy space with natural light and Central Park views is the perfect backdrop for Chef Vongerichten's shockingly original contemporary dishes, all of which underscore his mastery of French technique and his passion for seasonal ingredients and Asian influences. The menu changes seasonally, becoming a perpetual celebration of textures, flavors, and surprising combinations. Favorites include sea urchin with jalapeño on black bread, "Egg Caviar" (*sous vide* egg yolks on crisply toasted brioche with crème fraîche and a thick layer of caviar), and turbot in Challons sauce. Expect each course to be finished in front of you at the table, and, as one critic promises, "one, if not two or three, astonishing dishes provoking uncontrollable sighs or moans." The international wine list is award winning, dessert is four interpretations of a theme (such as citrus and herbs or chocolate), and the restaurant's long-standing consistency is ensured by Jean-Georges's brother, Director of Operations Philippe Vongerichten.

CRITICS' TIPS

In late summer, come just before twilight to watch the stars come out over Central Park.

If you can't get reservations in advance, drop in at 2 p.m. and see if there's a table available.

Consider trying Nougatine, the restaurant's adjoining bistro, which offers New York's best lunch bargain.

TRUMP HOTEL CENTRAL PARK
1 CENTRAL PARK WEST
NEW YORK, NY 10023
212.299.3900
WWW.JEAN-GEORGES.COM

UNI (SEA URCHIN) AND *IKURA GUNKAN (SALMON ROE) MAKI*

KURUMAZUSHI

[JAPANESE] Though the nondescript, midtown office building and unsteady elevator ride might not seem to bode well for an evening of exceptional dining, all doubts disappear after one bite at unassuming Kurumazushi. Expect no bells and whistles here. Rather, whether at the simple, blonde-wood bar, the handful of additional tables, or in the small private dining room, simply indulge in top-notch *edo*, or *nigiri*-style sushi and sashimi that's best described as superb. You can order à la carte, but if you select the *omakase*, or chef's choice, Chef Toshihiro Uezu will, with little fanfare, astonish you with an array of fresh dishes. Depending on the season and availability, a meal might include fresh salmon roe, rich monkfish liver paté, delicate yellowtail, or impossibly sweet shrimp. Uezu's reputation for *toro* is well deserved, and the quality of his sushi rice is worthy of study and worship. The chef and his welcoming staff delight in sharing their knowledge of the cuisine with novice diners. They also provide recommendations from their excellent saké selections, which perfectly complement the extraordinary raw fish dishes.

CRITICS' TIPS

Don't let the downmarket environs confuse you. Prices are high and on par with quality sushi in Tokyo.

Request to sit at the sushi bar or in one of the private rooms.

If you're cost conscious, keep in mind that menu choices are more reasonable than the omakase *but include the same superb-quality fish.*

7 EAST 47TH STREET, 2ND FLOOR
NEW YORK, NY 10017
212.317.2802
WWW.KURUMAZUSHI.COM

SPINOSINI WITH CLAMS, *SEPPIA*, AND CHILE

MAREA

♛ 🔑

[COASTAL ITALIAN] In his paean to fresh pasta and seafood, revered chef Michael White marries the two in spectacular fashion in an equally alluring setting. Rosewood-paneled walls, windowsills lined with stilted seashells, and a bar carved from Egyptian onyx provide a fitting backdrop for White's gorgeously composed Mediterranean seafood dishes. The long list of oysters, caviar, and creative crudo and seafood antipasti changes seasonally, but a meal might kick off with octopus crudo with chile oil, lemon, and parsley or sea urchin wrapped in lard and sprinkled with sea salt. Even more exciting are the renowned pastas. Made in-house and by hand, they might take the shape of fusilli with red wine–braised octopus and creamy bone marrow or equally exceptional spaghetti with crab, Santa Barbara sea urchin, and fresh basil. For the avowed carnivore, the grilled Creekstone 50-day-aged sirloin is a satisfying alternative to the bounty from the sea. Rounding out the experience are an award-winning wine list, including a dazzling array of rosés, and dramatic desserts like *strati di cioccolato*, a heady mix of textures and flavors from coffee to salted caramel to dark chocolate.

CRITICS' TIPS

If you can get it, a great table is in the corner, below street level, and closest to Columbus Circle.

While the menu is recommended as a four-course fixed-price affair, you may order à la carte.

Consider skipping the fish entrées and have one of the glorious pasta dishes as a main course.

240 CENTRAL PARK SOUTH
NEW YORK, NY 10019
212.582.5100
WWW.MAREA-NYC.COM

TODAY'S TASTEMAKERS

With today's heightened focus on top-quality ingredients and chefs growing and even butchering their own food, the restaurant industry is quickly cultivating a new breed of resident expert. The following are just a few of today's specialists contributing to the evolution of restaurant dining.

Forager: Restaurant foragers, such as those employed by Chez Panisse (p. 183) and Noma (p. 201), don't necessarily spend all of their time trudging through the woods in search of wild mushrooms, though sometimes they do. Most often, they are likely to hunt and gather the best ingredients by developing relationships with farmers, butchers, and beekeepers and buying directly from them.

Gardener: Berkeley's Alice Waters might have been among the first U.S. chefs known for growing her own produce, but these days restaurant gardeners are becoming as common as sommeliers. Green thumbs managing restaurant gardens can be found everywhere from California's The French Laundry (p. 185) to New York's Blue Hill at Stone Barns (p. 149) to Paris's L'Arpège (p. 21) to Austria's Steirereck (p. 205).

Cheese Steward: There's more to championing a restaurant's cheese selection than a great nose. Cheese stewards forge relationships with dairy and cheese suppliers and know everything there is to know about cheese, from the best sources to how to store and ripen them to how to best pair them with other foods and wines. Watch them work at restaurants like Paris's Taillevent (p. 57) and New York's Daniel (p. 157).

Mixologist: The renaissance of the cocktail, the popularity of small-batch artisanal spirits, and the use of fresh and unexpected ingredients have brought mixologists into vogue. No longer just a pretty face and a quick wit behind the bar, these gourmet bartenders are well versed in cocktail culture

A SERVER GATHERING HERBS FROM THE TISANE GARDEN
AT BLUE HILL AT STONE BARNS (P. 149)

and history—and through creative concoctions, they often make cocktail history of their own. Meanwhile, molecular mixologists are making their own mark, using high-tech gadgets to craft cocktails of foam, smoke, and essences at spots such as Chicago's Alinea (p. 177) and the U.K.'s The Fat Duck (p. 193).

Water Sommelier: We already pay top dollar for bottled water in grocery stores, so it's not much of a leap to anticipate the "water sommelier"—an expert arbiter of the world's best water—as the next new thing. It's already the case at First Floor in Berlin. This restaurant hired a water sommelier in 2009 and provided a list featuring more than 40 specialty waters, including Tasmanian rainwater and water tastings.

SEKI AJI (HORSE MACKEREL)

MASA

[JAPANESE] Following the tradition of Japan's most reputable *kappo-kaiseki* establishments, Manhattan's greatest sushi restaurant exemplifies the divinity that comes with a knowing use of restraint and artistry. In contrast to the bustling upscale mall in which it resides, the restaurant is serene and singular in its focal point—the 10-seat counter, which is made from a $60,000 slab of imported Japanese *hinoki* wood and lit to showcase the intricate, opulent presentations of Chef Masa Takayama. Masa got his start at one of Tokyo's top *edo*-style sushi restaurants before making a name for himself with Ginza Sushiko in Beverly Hills, and he takes his art to another level here. He and his staff craft the day's offerings from what's freshest and in season and serve them on handmade pottery, some of it cast by Chef Takayama, who works with a Japanese potter each year. Whether seated at the counter or a table, because the menu is *omakase*, you must leave the decisions to the master and savor the parade of astonishing preparations, perhaps including Takayama's delicate blowfish or famed *toro* tartare with caviar. Regardless, many critics agree there is no better place in New York City to discover what fish and sushi should taste like.

CRITICS' TIPS

Go in early winter, when blowfish is in season, for a special treat.

Sit at the counter for your first few visits to see the elegant ease of a master at work.

Don't hesitate to ask Chef Takayama for wine recommendations. He loves wine with sushi and knows his stuff. He and his sommelier can also point you to impossible-to-get sake from very small Japanese producers.

TIME WARNER CENTER
10 COLUMBUS CIRCLE, 4TH FLOOR
NEW YORK, NY 10019
212.823.9800
WWW.MASANYC.COM

SOFT-COOKED HEN EGG WITH CAVIAR, ONIONS, AND POTATO

MOMOFUKU KO

[NEW AMERICAN] This tiny, 12-seat laboratory remains the most intimate and ambitious enterprise in peripatetic chef David Chang's ever-expanding oeuvre. Relentlessly experimental and entirely market driven, Momofuku Ko combines French, Korean, Japanese, Scandinavian, Italian, and more in a cuisine that's thoroughly global and often memorable. Across the narrow, blonde-wood counter, you'll feel the heat of the grill as Executive Chef Sean Gray and his team craft each 10-course dinner menu. With bright lighting and no waitstaff, this destination relies on Chang's cuisine to hold the spotlight—and it does. *Amuses* like crackly pork rind give way to a parade of other unexpected dishes, such as *sous vide* duck or his signature foie gras "snow"—frozen goose liver shaved into an ice dust that one of our critics promises is nothing short of amazing. Desserts are no less imaginative; the aptly named cereal milk *panna cotta*, which has become one of Chang's trademark finales, mingles milk with corn flakes for its flavoring—as well as avocado purée to balance its sweetness. Successful and adventurous combinations such as this are what keeps Momofuko Ko pleasantly surprising.

CRITICS' TIPS

The only way to get a seat is to reserve online within a 10-day period for dinner and a 14-day period for lunch. Reservations are accepted every morning starting at 10 a.m.

Consider coming for lunch, when the longer and more expensive 16-course menu is offered—and expect it to take at least three hours.

Those with food allergies should check the selection beforehand, as the preset menu includes very few alternatives.

"ASHER BLUE": PIEDMONT HAZELNUT "GÉNOISE," ROYAL BLENHEIM
APRICOT, CELERY BRANCH, AND AGED BALSAMIC VINEGAR

PER SE

[CONTEMPORARY AMERICAN] One critic dubs this "The French Laundry east"—a reference to Owner-Chef Thomas Keller's other temple to the art of food in California's pastoral, romantic Napa Valley. With Per Se, Keller embraces his urban milieu, not least with the outstanding Columbus Circle views from the best window-front seats. A meal here is not just dinner; it's a sense-provoking culinary oratorio orchestrated with great aplomb. The dark, luxuriously spaced Adam D. Tihany–designed dining room showcases Chef Keller's aptitude for elevating American flavors through European technique. The multicourse menu, overseen by Keller and Chef de Cuisine Eli Kaimeh, features French Laundry classics (such as "Oysters and Pearls" and salmon cornets) as well as seasonal variations and new creations. Exquisitely presented, finished tableside, and occasionally affording a learning moment, perhaps through a sampler of salts or olive oils, each dish is pure culinary theater. But it's not all drama. Some offerings, such as deviled egg with truffle pop tart, illuminate Keller's humor, while a finale of exquisite sweets and a robust wine list exemplify Keller's perpetual strive for perfection.

CRITICS' TIPS

Reservations are very hard to get, but you can drop in for à la carte offerings in the salon, where reservations are not accepted.

Consider the vegetarian menu; Per Se is one of the few top restaurants in the world to offer an elaborate meat-free meal daily—and do it incredibly well.

After your meal, request to tour Keller's dream kitchen, which is bigger than the dining room.

TIME WARNER CENTER
10 COLUMBUS CIRCLE, 4TH FLOOR
NEW YORK, NY 10019
212.823.9335
WWW.PERSENY.COM

STEAMED LOBSTER WITH *UNI* MOUSSE IN A LOTUS WRAPPER, SMOKED *UNI*, AND CAVIAR

SOTO

[CONTEMPORARY JAPANESE SEAFOOD] With no sign outside, Soto is a hidden gem worth finding. Inside the simply elegant white room marked by a blonde-wood sushi bar, white-tablecloth-draped tables, and a large inlaid red circle on a wall, Chef Sotohiro Kosugi and several assistants craft an inventive, modern menu that emphasizes fresh fish. Whether you come for sushi, small plates or "kitchen" menu, or the multicourse *omakase* menu, *uni* (sea urchin) is a must; wrapped in strands of squid and topped with fresh quail egg, it's an aesthetic and gastronomic triumph. Chef Kosugi has a masterful way with tartare as well, as evidenced by an extraordinary and distinctly fresh presentation of *toro* with avocado coulis, caviar, and spicy ponzu. Kosugi honed his craft as a third-generation sushi chef in a small Japanese fishing village before heading to the states. But his broiled New Zealand langoustine with a rich shiitake sauce proves that he's more than comfortable leveraging his Western environs, ingredients, and influences to our advantage. The wine list offers an impressive array of artisanal sakes.

CRITICS' TIPS

Sit at the sushi counter for the best view of the chef at work.

Whatever else you order, make a point of trying Kosugi's brilliant sushi. It's a benchmark all others should be held up to.

Don't pass up the seasonal dishes and daily specials. They tend to amaze.

357 6TH AVENUE
NEW YORK, NY 10014
212.414.3088

PHEASANT WITH SHALLOT, CIDER, AND BURNING OAK LEAVES

ALINEA

[MODERNIST] Everything about Alinea is revolutionary, as if Chef Grant Achatz wants to redefine what a restaurant can be. Consequently, an evening here feels more like a performance in which the kitchen, servers, and diners are all participants. The star, Chef Achatz, is a master of molecular gastronomy who astounds with a surprisingly balanced and satisfying, indescribably creative menu that might include such classics as Hot Potato, a thimble-size dish of hot potato soup over which, impaled on a pin, hang a slice of truffle, a tiny ball of potato, and a square of butter. Pull the pin, and the accoutrements drop into the soup. It's pure drama. Another masterpiece, Black Truffle Explosion, delivers on its promise with a gelled truffle-stock-filled ravioli that literally bursts in the mouth. In keeping with the unexpected, a course might be served on a silicone tablecloth laid directly on the polished mahogany table, serving pieces and flatware have been custom designed for each dish, and servers are highly trained to guide you through the culinary wonderland. Accentuating the dinner theater trope, rather than accepting reservations, Alinea sells tickets for its tasting menu.

CRITICS' TIPS

If it's on the menu, try the Lamb 86, an 86-ingredient dish served with 64 composed garnishes—all colorful, all fantastically delicious, and served in little dots like old-fashioned ribbon candy.

Definitely opt for wine pairings, which astound in their range and compatibility.

Also try Next, Alinea's sister restaurant, which changes its menu every four months.

1723 NORTH HALSTED STREET
CHICAGO, IL 60614
312.867.0110
WWW.ALINEA-RESTAURANT.COM

RAVIOLI, PINE NUT, CARAMELIZED ONION, MATSUTAKE, AND LIME

[MODERN SEAFOOD] When Chef Matthew Kirkley couldn't get truly fresh seafood in Chicago, he brought the ocean to his town, literally. Behind the scenes at L2O, in two different tanks that mimic different bodies of water, Kirkley houses everything from Brittany blue lobsters to geoduck clams to California abalone, all in the name of fine dining. While guests seated in the modern dining room don't have a view of the makeshift oceans and their inhabitants, they certainly admire the results on the plate. Two different tasting menus (seven-course price fixed or twelve-course tasting) are impeccably and artfully composed each night. While they lean heavily on seafood, there is plenty of variation. Dishes might include ahi tuna tartare, whereby the tuna is tucked inside a perfect orb of avocado. A crab "chip" Old Bay pays homage to the chef's Baltimore childhood, while turbot with andouillette and matelote normande is a nod to his reverence for French culinary tastes and technique. Wine Director Richard Hanauer presides over an extraordinary collection of vintage Champagnes and a list rich with white Burgundies, which perfectly match the restaurant's myriad seafood offerings.

CRITICS' TIPS

Ask for a peak inside the kitchen so you can view the massive seafood tanks firsthand.

Don't be afraid to ask for wine suggestions. Hanauer and his staff are as helpful as they are knowledgeable.

2300 NORTH LINCOLN PARK WEST
CHICAGO, IL 60614
773.868.0002
L2ORESTAURANT.COM

OYSTER PORK BELLY KIMCHI

BENU

[CONTEMPORARY AMERICAN] Tucked into a tiny lane in San Francisco's South of Market district, Korean-born chef Corey Lee produces some of the city's most inventive, intricately prepared, and artfully plated cuisine. A former chef de cuisine at Thomas Keller's The French Laundry, Lee shares Keller's exacting standards and mastery of French technique. But his Asian-influenced contemporary American fare is entirely original. Midweek, an à la carte menu is offered, but to get a true sampling of the next generation of culinary sophistication, opt for the tasting menu with shockingly creative yet wholly balanced and satisfying East-West combinations. If it's available, try "salt and pepper squid"—a single airy chip crafted from squid, its ink, and tapioca flour that's dotted with minced squid and pickled serrano chile. More straightforward is the succulent pork rib eye "in the style of baked ham." Along with overseeing the restaurant's stark interior design, which is awash in wood and neutral tones, Chef Lee orchestrated the custom serving dishes and utensils to match his modern cuisine. But one of his best choices was appointing Yoon Ha as the dining room and beverage director; he crafts truly brilliant, unexpected pairings for every course—be it wine, beer, or even sparkling sake.

CRITICS' TIPS

Determine how you'd like to eat before booking a table; a 14- to 18-course tasting menu is offered every evening, but à la carte selections are only available on Tuesday, Wednesday, and Thursday.

Even if you don't order wine pairings, ask Yoon Ha for drink recommendations. You won't regret it.

Make a point of pausing outside the restaurant to watch the kitchen through the large exterior windows.

22 HAWTHORNE STREET
SAN FRANCISCO, CA 94105
415.685.4860
WWW.BENUSF.COM

AVOCADO AND MARINATED BEET SALAD WITH PURSLANE

CHEZ PANISSE

[CALIFORNIA] There is no other restaurant in the world quite like this Berkeley landmark, which has been a revered gastronomic destination for more than 40 years. Menus, which change nightly, feature gorgeously pristine, straightforward preparations of organic and sustainably grown and harvested ingredients. Though chefs have changed over the years, founder Alice Waters's guiding vision and passion, verging on obsession, for procuring the best possible local ingredients keeps the restaurant and its upstairs "café" on course. The cozy wood-paneled craftsman-style interior perfectly matches the food: not too fussy and utterly tasteful, with bountiful floral bouquets and bowls of fruit, and adjoining the surprisingly quiet open kitchen. Current chefs Jérôme Waag and Cal Peternell, each of whom oversees the kitchen for half of the year, show a variety of influences, but the menu generally leans toward the Mediterranean. As one critic says, "Though you might come here and discover, to your disappointment, that the main course is nothing but a lamb chop, then the lamb chop arrives, and you realize that it is the best one you've ever tasted, that it has completely changed your notion of what a lamb chop can be."

CRITICS' TIPS

Reserve wisely; early in the week the meals are less expensive, more rustic, and usually more interesting. On weekends the price goes up and menus become more staid.

Explore the wine list. The selection is almost entirely under $100 and includes wonderful Domaine Tempier wines from Bandol, France, which go decidedly well with the food.

Also consider trying the adjoining café, which is a more casual affair that's equally revered by critics and chefs.

1517 SHATTUCK AVENUE
BERKELEY, CA 94709
510.548.5525
WWW.CHEZPANISSE.COM

THOMAS FARM SQUAB WITH YELLOW PEACH, FENNEL BULB, PETITE ONIONS, AND NIÇOISE OLIVES

THE FRENCH LAUNDRY

[CONTEMPORARY AMERICAN] Though Thomas Keller's Napa Valley, California, jewel might be one of the most difficult restaurant reservations to get in the country, for serious food lovers it's one of the most worthwhile. Just over 20 years ago, Keller bought The French Laundry and became one of the most lauded chefs in the world, and his attention to detail hasn't waned. Within its intimate Wine Country setting, classical French culinary techniques continue to be parlayed into utterly rich and luxurious multicourse meals—all of which are plated to perfection, finished tableside, and explained in elaborate detail. Now presided over by Chef de Cuisine David Breeden, each day's menu is new. However, Keller classics, such as Macaroni and Cheese, Tongue in Cheek, and Oysters and Pearls—whose fanciful names belie their sophisticated underpinnings—have long been signature dishes. Meticulous about sourcing, Keller's kitchen serves produce only in season, only at its peak, much of it grown across the street in the restaurant's garden. Equally thoughtful and methodical is the service, which is overseen by General Manager Michael Minnillo. Diners should expect no mere meal but a culinary performance, one with multiple acts, surprise encores, and even optional garden-stroll intermissions.

CRITICS' TIPS

The restaurant's garden is not to be missed. Take a stroll after (or even during) your meal.

Don't skip the rolls and Vermont butter. They're remarkable.

There's never a bad time to eat here, but during the fall wine harvest is especially wonderful.

6640 WASHINGTON STREET
YOUNTVILLE, CA 94599
707.944.2380
WWW.FRENCHLAUNDRY.COM

TROUT, FORGOTTON HERBS, FIG RESIN, AND CHARRED CAULIFLOWER

THE RESTAURANT AT MEADOWOOD

[MODERN AMERICAN] An entirely original culinary journey awaits at this bucolic Napa Valley retreat where the pastoral surroundings provide the culinary inspiration and backdrop for Chef Christopher Kostow's inventive "Wine Country" cuisine. With no menu, guests are presented with a card listing various ingredients included in the evening's daily-changing eight- to nine-course fixed-price affair. Read it and the meal still remains a mystery. Every evening begins with a parade of whimsical one-bite amuse-bouches, but it's the following course where Kostow's talent truly shines. Dishes feature the freshest, in-season products plucked from nearby farms and the restaurant's gardens, and they are artistically composed in ways that literally echo the natural surroundings. Meanwhile, all the classic luxury offerings—such as veal, tuna, steak, and langoustines—are also well represented, only they appear in unexpected ways that defy description yet manage to be abundantly creative and wholly satisfying. Perfect wine pairings come from a nearly 1,100-bottle wine list composed largely of stellar California wines. Finally, a recent remodel ensures that the environs—replete with fine leather chairs, handsome dark wood, and comfortably spaced white-clothed tables—match the world-class food.

CRITICS' TIPS

Come before sunset in order to appreciate the spectacular view.

For the ultimate experience, reserve the exclusive $500-per-person kitchen counter and dine on a more elaborate menu in the heart of the kitchen action. Or, at a minimum, request a peek at the impressive, gleaming, 3,000-square-foot cooking space.

MEADOWOOD RESORT
900 MEADOWOOD LANE
ST. HELENA, CA 94574
707.967.1205
WWW.THERESTAURANTATMEADOWOOD.COM   UNITED STATES   **187**

STEAMED LANGOUSTINES, RAVIOLI, AND SPICY CONSOMMÉ

ALAIN DUCASSE AT THE DORCHESTER

[CONTEMPORARY FRENCH] Famed chef Alain Ducasse brings his signature French haute cuisine to a stunning London setting. Patrick Jouin designed the sumptuous space around a sparkling centerpiece, the "Table Lumière"—a table for six shrouded by a ceiling-to-floor veil of 4,500 shimmer fiber optics. Though dramatic texture and flair are the cornerstone of the restaurant's design, pure, elemental French cuisine is the focus on the plate. Championed by Chef Jocelyn Herland, superb dishes are made from the best local and seasonal ingredients, from the light and welcoming *gougères* to the final *macaron*. His roast chicken—with an almost frothy texture and fragrant truffle sauce—elevates the classic comfort food to luxurious heights. Roasted venison rib with chestnut and quince is tender and piquant. Scottish langoustine is steamed and opulently adorned with caviar or black truffle. Even a simple wild sea bass with braised endive imparts an exquisite and surprising complexity of flavor. Sommelier Vincent Pastorello offers wonderful wine pairings and suggestions from the Franco-centric cellar, while dessert—particularly his famed and notable *Baba au Rhum*—is an event in and of itself.

CRITICS' TIPS

Although a two-course menu is available, try the tasting menu for a terrific sampling of Ducasse's legendary cuisine.

If langoustine is offered, definitely order it.

Dessert here really is mandatory; don't even think of skipping it.

53 PARK LANE
LONDON W1K 1QA
+44 (0)20 7629 8866
WWW.ALAINDUCASSE-DORCHESTER.COM

QUAIL JELLY, CRAYFISH CREAM, CHICKEN LIVER PARFAIT, TRUFFLE TOAST, AND OAK MOSS

THE FAT DUCK

[MODERN BRITISH] After nearly two decades, this British stalwart still annually receives the highest accolades—whether as "Best Restaurant in the U.K." or even in the world. Much of this is due to its self-taught chef-owner Heston Blumenthal, who is widely praised for helming the molecular gastronomy movement—though he proclaims to loathe that term. Call it what you will: Blumenthal uses modern technology and a multisensory culinary approach to create sometimes revolutionary dishes. His famed Mad Hatter's Tea, a mock turtle soup complete with a gold-wrapped gelatinized bouillon pocket watch that dissolves before your eyes when immersed in hot water, visually re-creates the tea party in *Alice in Wonderland*. But the sophisticated flavors of this tea party don't summon childhood nostalgia; instead they inspire food fantasies to dream about for years to come. The menu is often rife with unexpected creations, such as snail porridge, powdered Anjou pigeon, chicken liver parfait, or jelly of quail (pictured at left). But despite its elite reputation and adventurous ingredients and presentation, the Fat Duck is not an overly fancy affair. Situated in a residential neighborhood in the small village of Bray, which is only 50 minutes from London by train, the minimalist décor, with original oak beams, nods to the everyday English pub it once was.

CRITICS' TIPS

If you've never been here before, consider ordering the tasting menu, which highlights many of Blumenthal's trademark creations.

Expect to spend three to four hours if you opt for the 14-course price-fixed menu; it's a marathon event.

Consider coming for lunch; it's the best time of day to experience the environs.

HIGH STREET, BRAY
BERKSHIRE SL6 2AQ
+44 (0)1628 580 333
WWW.THEFATDUCK.CO.UK

ROASTED LOIN OF LAMB STUFFED WITH AUBERGINE CONFIT AND GRILLED PINE KERNELS "GÂTEAU" OF MOUSSAKA AND A LIGHT SAFFRON-FLAVORED JUS

THE WATERSIDE INN

[CLASSIC FRENCH] After more than four decades serving spectacular French food in a stunning Thames River waterfront setting, the Waterside Inn is no less than a national treasure. Founding chef-owner Michel Roux's magnificent attention to detail has resulted in a dining room both composed and relaxed, a place where classic cooking, formal presentation, and astute combinations of taste and texture are celebrated. Alain Roux, who inherited the throne from his now-retired father, maintains Michel's lofty standards. His masterful hand with seafood is evident in lobster medallions in white port sauce, a silky indulgence of the best kind. But his talents aren't limited to the sea. To wit: His roasted Challandais duck for two is a magnificent dish. An *escalope de foie gras chaud à la Grenobloise* delivers a remarkable contrast between the melting foie gras and the attendant morsels of crisp bread and capers. Even the "teardrop of milk chocolate mousse" dessert exhibits unexpected complexity with intermingled flavors of caramel, mango, and passion fruit. The wine list is extensive and entirely French, offering 1,000 selections, and service here mirrors the food: highly polished without a trace of pretension.

CRITICS' TIPS

With river views from nearly every seat in the house, try to book in summer when the vistas are particularly lovely.

Roux's training as a pâtissier makes saving room for soufflé mandatory.

Book one of the inn's rooms so you can do justice to the vast wine list.

FERRY ROAD, BRAY
BERKSHIRE SL6 2AT
+44 (0)1628 620691
WWW.WATERSIDE-INN.CO.UK

GRILLED CORNISH MACKEREL AND PICKLED *MOULI* WITH
HONEY-SOY DRESSING

LE MANOIR AUX QUAT'SAISONS

[MODERN FRENCH] Le Manoir aux Quat'Saisons may occupy a windowed dining room in a fifteenth-century English manor house turned boutique luxury hotel, but it might as well be in France. Here, imaginative French food is crafted from fresh local produce picked from the property's two-acre garden at its prime by Chef-Patron Raymond Blanc and Executive Head Chef Gary Jones. At the helm since 1999, Jones exhibits Old-World-meets-New-World style that is evident throughout the seasonal menu. Although there is an à la carte menu, the six-, seven-, or nine-course tasting menus provide better opportunities to sample the inventive dishes. When in season and available, opt for the roast grouse with cabbage, bacon, and blackberry jus. Also particularly elegant is the wild Cornish brill oyster with cucumber, surrounded by brilliant green wasabi beurre blanc. If you're here in winter, you might have the luxury of completing your meal with mulled winter fruits with cinnamon ice cream. Accompanying the diverse menu is a 1,000-bottle global wine list, 60 percent of which is French, as well as a knowledgeable sommelier to help narrow the choices.

CRITICS' TIPS

Indoors, no table is better than the next, but the outdoor patio is ideal for an aperitif on a balmy summer evening.

Save some time to meander through the estate's two-acre potager (vegetable garden) and orchard.

If you want a bargain and a lighter, multicourse meal, come for the five-course, fixed-price lunch.

CHURCH ROAD
GREAT MILTON, OXFORD OX44 7PD
+44 (0)184 427 8881
WWW.MANOIR.COM

THE "FARM-TO-TABLE" EVOLUTION

The farm-to-table relationship is so natural that it's hard to call it a trend. Yet despite regional exceptions, such as Kyoto's *Kyo-ryōri* cuisine—which is rooted in the Zen belief of living in the moment—the connection between fresh local ingredients and dinner hasn't always been so obvious or celebrated.

In the United States, Alice Waters is credited with fostering the movement, which is based on the notion that cooking should use only the finest, freshest sustainably and locally produced seasonal ingredients. Promoting organic farmers and ranchers and hiring foragers to find the best produce has been her passion since 1971, when her iconic restaurant Chez Panisse (p. 183) opened.

In synch with Alice Waters, the Slow Food movement began in Europe in the 1980s in response to a proposed McDonald's opening near Rome's Spanish Steps. Today, it's a worldwide effort that focuses on preserving family farms, heirloom varieties, and local and traditional food products along with their lore and preparations.

The most recent trend within the farm-to-table movement—kitchen gardens—is being spearheaded by some of the world's top chefs, including Alain Passard of Paris's L'Arpège (p. 21), René Redzepi of Copenhagen's Noma (p. 201), and Daniel Patterson of San Francisco's Coi (p. 250). Thus far, Passard has taken the concept the furthest, creating seasonal menus crafted only from his own produce. Redzepi and Patterson focus on foraging for wild ingredients, and Redzepi has gone so far as to work with historians, botanists, and philosophers to unearth native ingredients. Coupled with the popularity of farmers' markets, the farm-to-table trend is likely to influence home and restaurant cooking for the foreseeable future.

TOP 10 MANAGERS, DIRECTORS, OR MAÎTRE D'HÔTELS

While the chef deservedly receives much of the credit for a restaurant's success, there's more to a truly exceptional dining experience than what arrives on the plate. Here we honor the top professionals who make everything in the front of house and beyond—from reservations to service to operations—a revered art form and an affair to remember.

Ben Chekroun
Maître d'Hôtel
Le Bernardin
New York, NY, USA

Hélène Cousin
Restaurant Manager
L'Arpège
Paris, France

Frédéric Kaiser
Restaurant Manager
Epicure
Paris, France

Hubert Schwermer
Maître d'Hôtel
Restaurant Guy Savoy
Paris, France

Michael Minnillo
General Manager
The French Laundry
Yountville, CA, USA

Hervé Parmentier
Maître d'Hôtel
Pierre Gagnaire
Paris, France

Christophe Rohat
Maître d'Hôtel
L'Astrance
Paris, France

Pierre Siue
General Manager
Daniel
New York, NY, USA

Pascal Vettoux
Maître d'Hôtel
L'Ambroisie
Paris, France

Philippe Vongerichten
Director of Operations
Jean-Georges
New York, NY, USA

PICKLED VEGETABLES WITH SMOKED BONE MARROW

NOMA

[LOCAL/SEASONAL] You might not expect to find one of the world's most astonishing and cutting-edge restaurants tucked into a converted eighteenth-century Copenhagen food warehouse. But within this unpretentious waterfront space, the globally heralded chef René Redzepi performs his culinary opera, overseeing—encouraging—the collision of modernism and locavorism. Having exhaustively researched the fruits and vegetables of his native country, Redzepi puts to rest the myth of Scandinavia as produce deficient. In fact, along with an on-staff forager, he himself searches for and plucks much of what he serves. His seasonal, daily-changing tasting menu depends wholly on what he and his forager find; it might include live ants or tiny fjord shrimp, deep-fried lichen, or sautéed moldy barley terrine—all startling yet superb. Brace for adventure: Even the trademark fried egg—which involves the diner cooking a wild duck egg in hay oil at the table and enjoying it with just-foraged herbs and a lump of goat butter—is no simple dish but an outstandingly complex journey of flavors. Fruit-and-vegetable-juice pairings are further evidence that as the world undergoes a culinary revolution, Redzepi is helping lead the charge.

CRITICS' TIPS

Reservations are difficult, but be persistent. Redzepi's Twitter feed (@ReneRedzepiNoma) often mentions openings.

Try for a table by the windows with a spectacular view onto Copenhagen Harbor.

Eat very, very lightly the day before a meal at Noma. Your stomach will need the room.

STRANDGADE 93
DK-1401 COPENHAGEN K
+45 3296 3297
NOMA.DK

SIMMERED "CORNED-BEEF" MÜRITZ LAMB WITH FRANKFURT-STYLE
SAUCE, POTATO, AND EGG

AQUA

[CONTEMPORARY GERMAN] Located inside the Ritz-Carlton in Germany's industrial town of Wolfsburg, which is also home to Volkswagen's headquarters, Aqua has become one of the region's main draws, primarily due to the artistry of its renowned chef, Sven Elverfeld. Elverfeld's singular genius and mission is reflected in the strikingly graphic contemporary German dishes he creates: at once incredibly simple yet cleverly refined, and exploring a decidedly German taste spectrum of smoke, sourness, and salt tempered by occasional Italian or Spanish inflections. Served in a stark, angular dining space punctuated by bold colors, art deco touches, and floor-to-ceiling windows, his multicourse fixed-price-only dining format might include a spoon tasting of meatballs, perhaps preceded by a miniature *currywurst*. Palate-cleansing sorbets are served atop an oversize ice block, while black olives might arrive coated with caramel. An ice cream trio, perhaps blackberry, jasmine, and sour milk over a dash of chocolate mousse, might finish the meal, while a wide selection of international wines allows for perfect complements to each course.

CRITICS' TIPS

If you're not staying in the area, take the one-hour express train ride from Berlin. This young chef's interpretation of contemporary German cuisine makes the trip worthwhile.

Make sure to arrive hungry. Tasting menu options range from four to nine courses, and the entire table must agree on the same number of courses.

Don't pass up the opportunity to explore the wide selection of German offerings on the diverse wine list.

THE RITZ-CARLTON, WOLFSBURG
PARKSTRASSE 1
38440 WOLFSBURG
+49 5361 606056
WWW.RESTAURANT-AQUA.COM

HOCHSCHWAB VENISON WITH BABY MARCHFELD ARTICHOKES,
MUSTARD HERB, AND ORANGE BLOSSOM

STEIRERECK

[CONTEMPORARY AUSTRIAN] One of the finest places in Vienna to experience modern Austrian food, Steirereck is located in an opulently restored light-filled German art nouveau pavilion in the city's Stadtpark, gorgeously situated along the riverbank. The landmark setting is a fitting backdrop for Chef Heinz Reitbauer and his wife, Birgit, who elevate their country's traditional cuisine through the use of contemporary techniques and sustainably produced local ingredients, some of which are grown in their own gardens. Reitbauer, whose family has owned this Austrian jewel for more than 40 years, admirably doesn't defer to French cuisine, insisting instead on reimagining Austrian staples. The menus vary according to the season, but you're likely to find a classic Wiener schnitzel with parsley potatoes on the lunch menu, while free-range pork with elderberry, fennel, and Cox apple is a popular favorite on the autumn evening tasting menu. After dinner, many carts are wheeled to the table proffering every possible temptation, including breads, cheeses, sublime Viennese pastries, and cigars. The restaurant's 35,000-bottle cellar, composed mainly of Austrian and Styrian wine, and a large selection of after-dinner drinks make this spot a popular post-performance destination among the city's opera-goers.

CRITICS' TIPS

Don't pass up the outstanding cheese course; more than 120 types from 13 different countries are on offer.

Visit during the summer and dine alfresco on the terrace.

If you can't get a table at Steirereck, try its downstairs sister restaurant, Meierei, that, in addition to its vast collection of cheese, serves pastries and a less-expensive café menu in a more casual setting.

STADTPARK
AM HEUMARKT 2A
1030 VIENNA
+43 (1) 713 31 68
WWW.STEIRERECK.AT

ROAST SUCKLING PIG WITH MUSTARD FOAM AND COFFEE POWDER

LE CALANDRE

[ITALIAN] Chef Massimiliano Alajmo took over his long-standing family business just two years after he was old enough to vote, and in less than a decade he turned it into one of the world's top food destinations. His parents, Erminio and Rita, first opened Le Calandre in 1983 and passed on the restaurant to their son when he was 20 years old. Eight years later, Alajmo became one of the youngest chefs to garner international fame among food lovers and critics throughout the world. His seasonal fare is hearty and often traditional, but always with a notable and original twist—such as a beignet injected with tomato juice, ravioli filled with pistachio tofu, or a roast suckling pig accompanied by coffee powder (pictured at left). Underscoring the ingenuity of today's generation, Le Calandre's 100-plus-page wine list is presented on an iPad and organized by grape varietal, origin, and price. Le Calandre also remains a family business; Chef Alajmo relies on his brother, Raf—who helped redesign the restaurant and serves as the company's CEO—while his parents and sister remain involved as well.

CRITICS' TIPS

Check the website's "Carpe Diem" section for fantastic values, such as half off a lunchtime tasting menu.

If available, don't miss the signature "grande classico" saffron risotto dusted with licorice, cuttlefish cappuccino, or "Chocolate Game" dessert.

If desired, ask for help navigating the wine list, which includes some terrific bargains.

VIA LIGURIA 1
35030 SARMEOLA DI RUBANO, PROVINCE OF
PADUA
+39 (0)49 633000
WWW.ALAJMO.IT

TENDERLOIN OF PIEDMONT VEAL WITH FIELD FLOWER
AND CHAMOMILE CRUST

IL LUOGO DI AIMO E NADIA

[CREATIVE ITALIAN] In a less fashionable neighborhood of Italy's fashion capital, Aimo and Nadia Moroni have been steadily turning out some of Milan's most notable dishes for more than half a century. The couple's 40-seat restaurant, featuring painted works and a sculptural installation by Paolo Ferrari and Simona Riboni, has become an absolute destination even for jaded locals. With a deft touch and a dedication to the best seasonal ingredients, Chefs Fabio Pisani and Alessandro Negrini take classic Italian cooking and tweak it in the most marvelous ways. A sumptuous starter of tartare features paper-thin slices of Piedmontese veal dressed with hazelnut shavings and paste, aged balsamic vinegar, and a buckwheat biscuit. Pastas are homemade and star in dishes such as the signature spaghetti with green onion and hot pepper sauce, a dish often copied but never matched. The chefs use seasonal ingredients like quince, lemongrass, and fennel flowers in fish and meat dishes as well, though the pâté of duck and pigeon liver with white truffle cream relies on more traditional components for its outstanding results. Among the restaurant's many other charms are Aimo's daughter, Stefania, the "soul of Aimo e Nadia" and their exceptional wine list.

CRITICS' TIPS

Despite its slightly out-of-the-way location on the outskirts of Milan, Il Luogo fills up fast, so book several weeks in advance.

For a broad spectrum of Pisani and Negrini's cuisine, order the tasting menu—and corresponding wine pairings, if desired.

VIA PRIVATA RAIMONDO MONTECUCCOLI, 6
20147 MILAN
+39 (0)2 416886
WWW.AIMOENADIA.COM

ORANGE-SCENTED SCALLOPS WITH JULIENNE OF LEEKS

OSTERIA ALLE TESTIERE

[ITALIAN SEAFOOD] The rustic atmosphere at this tiny trattoria tucked into a quiet Venetian street near the Campo Santa Maria Formosa belies the sophisticated dining experience that accompanies it. Nine simple tables are virtual blank canvases for Chef Bruno Gavagnin's extraordinary seasonal and local Italian fare prepared with a hint of modernity in his impossibly tiny kitchen. Together with Co-Owner and Sommelier Luca Di Vita, Gavagnin serves straightforward, yet consistently delicious coastal favorites— gnocchi with *calamaretti*, ricotta ravioli spiked with aromatic citrus and served amid fresh scallops, and fresh grilled sea bass, to name a few. The scampi *alla busara,* featuring delicate shrimp in a tomato-based sauce redolent of cinnamon, has made this trattoria a local favorite and burgeoning international darling. The menu here changes daily, if not hourly, and is wholly dependent on the seafood caught that day in nearby Venetian waters. Di Vita helps navigate a small but compelling and mostly Italian wine list, with an impressive selection of local whites. Desserts, such as crème brûlée, tiramisu, or homemade ginger-and-vanilla gelato, provide a perfect finale at this classic Italian *salotto*.

CRITICS' TIPS

With only nine tables and two seatings per night, it's imperative to reserve well in advance.

If razor clams are on the menu, don't pass them up.

While the wine list is wonderful, if you're on a budget you can confidently order the house wine.

CALLE DEL MONDO NOVO, 5801
30122 VENICE
+39 (0)415 227 220
WWW.OSTERIALLETESTIERE.IT

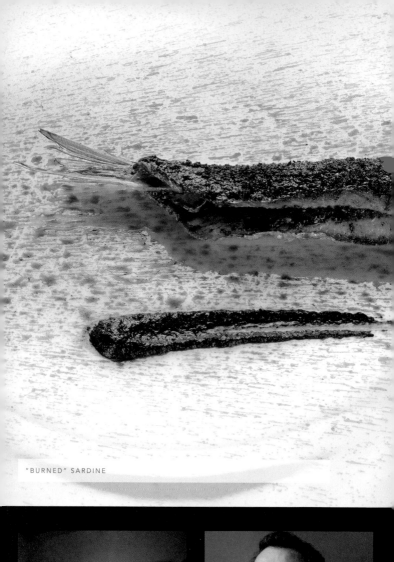

"BURNED" SARDINE

OSTERIA FRANCESCANA

[MODERN ITALIAN] In a land steeped in tradition, Chef Massimo Bottura turns the institution of Italian food on its head. With nods to both the noble local ingredients and the greats of modernist cuisine, he combines a bit of art and theater, classic Italian, and modernist cooking techniques to create food as whimsical as it is satisfying. Two main dining rooms with walls adorned with contemporary and experimental art by international artists provide the first hint that this won't be your average red-sauce Italian experience. He often employs deconstructivist tactics, so that "pumpkin ravioli" isn't ravioli at all, but balls of frothy pumpkin filling adrift in a broth of Parmesan rinds. His famed "Five Ages of Parmigiano Reggiano" explores the variety of textures and temperatures that can be cajoled from the Italian staple, from creamy to crisp to an ethereal "air." There are some nods to the past, such as his Modenese tortellini, a dish derived from memories of his grandmother's tortellini, and his Bolognese sauce, which tastes of generations. Still, foie gras *macarons* with foie gras marshmallows, and iced basil with buffalo mozzarella powder, are powerful reminders that, in Bottura's hands, everything old is entirely new.

CRITICS' TIPS

If you're a mushroom lover, plan a visit in the fall when seasonal fungi are at their peak—and employed here masterfully.

Be daring and try the constantly evolving Sensations tasting menu. These are the dishes currently under construction in Bottura's "experimental kitchen."

BABY OCTOPUS AND ITS INK

ASADOR ETXEBARRI

[TRADITIONAL BASQUE] In an old, stone building in the tiny Basque village of Bizkaia, self-taught chef Victor Arguinzoniz presides over a stove-free kitchen, using two wood-fired ovens and his custom grill to cook everything from appetizers to desserts. Taking this simple notion and method to its extreme, Chef Arguinzoniz combines only the best seasonal ingredients and a variety of woods—olive, oak, apple—to infuse his dishes with sublime and very subtle hints of smoke and to create astonishingly complex food. If you want insight into the meal ahead, the tasting menu won't help much. It lists only ingredients for each course: perhaps "baby octopus, sweet onions" for one, "anchovies" for another. Of course, the results are elaborate. Anchovies, for example, arrive boned, slightly charred, and smoky with a garnish of lightly dressed arugula, while sweet-onion confit complements the texture and taste of delicately grilled octopus. Even condensed-milk ice cream and flan get a turn on the grill, with brilliant results. Like the food, the restaurant is rustic and charming, with service to match, while views of verdant mountains and the quaint village command nearly as much attention as the food.

CRITICS' TIPS

Etxebarri is famously difficult to find. Use the directions from the restaurant's website and leave yourself plenty of driving time.

Try the tasting menu. It's an excellent way to experience Arguinzoniz's deft hand with a wide variety of dishes.

If the weather is good, sit outside among Spanish moss and leafy trees.

PLAZA SAN JUAN, 1
48291 ATXONDO, BIZKAIA
+34 94 658 30 42
WWW.ASADORETXEBARRI.COM

CHARCOAL-GRILLED KING PRAWN WITH KING-PRAWN SAND, INK, AND ROCKS, FRIED LEGS, HEAD JUICE, AND KING PRAWN ESSENCE

EL CELLER DE CAN ROCA

[MODERN SPANISH] Run by three brothers—Chef Joan, Patissier Jordi, and Sommelier Josep Roca—and located in an old stone villa 60 miles north of Barcelona in the medieval town of Girona, El Celler de Can Roca serves some of the finest modern, yet never overwrought regional food in Spain. The triangular wood-and-glass dining room oriented around a minimalist atrium creates a warm and inviting canvas for the wildly creative Catalan cuisine coming out of the kitchen. Evidence of cutting-edge techniques can be found in every dish, including an elderflower infusion with cherries and smoked sardine, which one of our critics found utterly memorable. However, kitchen sorcery is used only to enhance flavors and ingredients, never merely for show. Exceptionality extends to the sweet finales, which, if you're lucky, will include beautiful, innovative deconstructed desserts inspired by famous perfumes; they epitomize triumphant culinary innovation. Apt for a restaurant nestled in a country known for wine, the wine trolley toting an encyclopedic list provides extensive choices.

CRITICS' TIPS

If it's on the menu, don't pass up the salt cod brandade made with salt cod tripe; it's a traditional rustic Catalan dish elevated to the truly spectacular.

If you can, visit in the spring or fall, when it's ideal to stroll the town of Girona before or after your meal.

CAN SUNYER, 48
17007 GIRONA
+34 972 222 157
WWW.CELLERCANROCA.COM

RAVIOLI OF AROMATIC VEGETABLES

MUGARITZ

[CREATIVE] Mugaritz is one of Spain's finest practitioners of "techno-emotional" molecular gastronomy. Nestled in a rustic farmhouse in the Basque countryside about 10 miles outside of San Sebastian, it's run by Andoni Luis Aduriz, one of the country's most inventive young chefs who, along with his battalion of cooks, is constantly pushing the envelope, turning out thought-provoking deconstructed cuisine that's designed to evoke emotion and a sense of place. ("Mugaritz" is the merging of the Spanish words for the region's popular oak tree and "frontier.") A meal begins outside on the patio overlooking the verdant hills and herb gardens with a drink and a few light *amuse-bouches*, before settling down inside to a progression of dazzling, stunningly original small plates, starting with edible "paper" seasoned with olive paste. Examples of the kitchen's technical wizardry are everywhere, including the trademark "edible stones"—baked potatoes cooked in a thin lining of white clay to resemble granite rocks served over a bed of edible sand. According to one of our critics, the playful dish mimics the effect of biting into a river rock—without the broken teeth. Like the menu, the wine list reflects the local terroir with a fine selection of Spanish offerings, with international offerings sprinked in, and the staff is notably hospitable.

CRITICS' TIPS

Visit during the fall when the foliage is full of color and the chef turns out interesting dishes showcasing mushrooms, wild plants, and game.

Reservations are customarily required months in advance, but call back frequently. If you're lucky, you'll be able to take advantage of a cancellation.

Don't worry about where you sit; every seat is a good one, thanks to large windows that make you feel part of the forest setting.

OTZAZULUETA BASERRIA, ALDURA ALDEA 20
20100 ERRENTERIA, GIPUZKOA
+34 943 522 455
WWW.MUGARITZ.COM

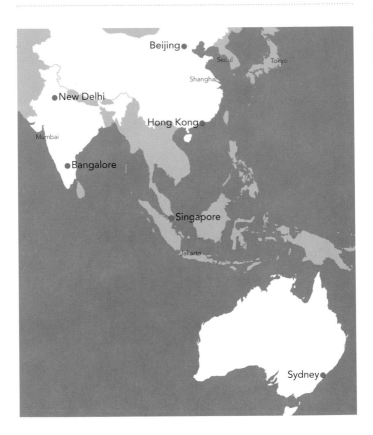

DEEP-FRIED LANGOUSTINE

FAMILY LI IMPERIAL CUISINE

[CHINESE] Tucked into a residential neighborhood behind Beijing's Imperial Palace, the Li family restaurant may not look like much from the exterior, but step inside and you'll dine, quite literally, like royalty. Family patriarch and restaurant founder Li Shanlin's son, Li Xiao Lin, cooks recipes his great-great-grandfather collected while running the household for the imperial court of the Qing Dynasty. Though the recipes were later destroyed by the Red Guard, Li memorized hundreds of them and spent years re-creating them. In an elegant space decorated with ornate, carved-wood screens and damask tablecloths, Li and his progeny pride themselves on serving faithfully executed Imperial Palace cuisine. The menu changes according to what's fresh and available each day (so the tiny dish of egg custard containing steamed snow frog oil won't appear often), yet among the myriad appetizers that always arrive with the meal are likely to be deep-fried langoustine (pictured at left), a superb roast pork, cold chicken in a sauce of ginger and Sichuan pepper, or pork and Napa cabbage soup. Peking duck and tea-smoked pork are equally exceptional and epitomize Chinese fine dining at its best.

CRITICS' TIPS

If possible, dine here twice and order different dishes each time. You'll be overwhelmed by the variety of Chinese cuisine.

Reservations are a must, so call well in advance.

If you visit in winter, dress warmly. The restaurant tends to get cold.

11 YANG FANG HUTONG
DE NEI DA JIE, XI CHENG DISTRICT
+86 10 66180107
WWW.BEIJINGLIJIACAI.OINSITE.CN

SAUTÉED CRABMEAT AND CRAB YOLK WITH CHINESE KALE

FOOK LAM MOON

[CANTONESE] The flagship and original location of what is now a string of outposts in China and Japan, Fook Lam Moon has been a Hong Kong institution for more than four decades. Of its many famous Cantonese dishes, the restaurant's signature crispy chicken is more than enough to lure diners from around the globe. Its crisp, well-seasoned skin and accompanying lemon-juice dip prompted one of our critics to dub it "one of the world's best chicken dishes." But regulars know there's much more to enjoy within the unassuming old-world second-floor dining room. All dishes are prepared in traditional fashion using the best ingredients, from the abundant shark-fin offerings—there are more than a dozen—to the abalone and bird's nest. Must-haves include braised Japanese dried abalone, lotus-wrapped fried rice, and the restaurant's famed bird's nest soup—dense, sweet, and winningly served in a coconut shell. Dim sum, also among the best in Hong Kong, is served daily and presents an excellent alternative to the extravagant tasting menus as well as an opportunity to enjoy an extremely wide variety of small dishes in one sitting.

CRITICS' TIPS

Visit at least twice while you're in Hong Kong. The first time, order dim sum à la carte and try the signature chicken. The second time, order the chef's fixed-price tasting menu.

Hundreds of staff members have been here for decades. Take advantage of their expertise and ask for recommendations.

Make sure to try the crab dishes and barbecued pig.

NEWMAN HOUSE
35-45 JOHNSTON ROAD
WANCHAI, HONG KONG
+852 2866 0663
WWW.FOOKLAMMOON-GRP.COM/EN/
HONGKONG/HOME.ASP

BRAISED SHORT RIBS WITH BARBECUE SAUCE

SUN TUNG LOK

[CANTONESE] For more than four decades, Sun Tung Lok has been famed in Hong Kong and beyond for both its delicate, traditional Cantonese dim sum and its handling of the triumverate of Chinese luxury staples: shark's fin, abalone, and bird's nest. Family run since 1969, the restaurant currently resides in a strip mall, a humble address that hides an elegant interior—muted tones, crisp tablecloths, and subtly baroque wallpaper. Only available at lunch, dim sum and à la carte menus are an embarrassment of riches, from braised goose web to hairy crab to crispy bacon spring rolls. Shrimp dumplings offer flavor as well as precision, each one perfectly pleated before steaming. The roast suckling pig—a masterpiece of Cantonese cuisine, with its crisp skin, shrimp stuffing, and perfectly flavored plum sauce—is everything the dish should be. Along with the braised shark's fin soup, it has brought Chef Yung Chan a considerable degree of renown.

CRITICS' TIPS

Expect a larger bill than you might receive at many Chinese and dim-sum houses. Prices here reflect the quality.

Don't miss the braised goose web or hairy crab.

SHOP 4D, MIRAMAR SHOPPING CENTRE
132 NATHAN ROAD, TSIM SHA TSUI,
KOWLOON, HONG KONG
+852 2152 1417
WWW.SUNTUNGLOK.COM.HK

BARRAH KEBAB

BUKHARA

[NORTHWEST FRONTIER INDIAN] New Delhi's most venerated restaurant has been a favorite of restaurant critics, well-heeled travelers, and heads of state since its 1978 opening. The wood-and-stone-wall dining room, outfitted with sofas and wood-slab stools, offers a fittingly rustic setting for traditional yet upscale Northwest Frontier cuisine. The restaurant prides itself on serving the same menu since the day it opened, and for good reason: Its signature kebabs are considered the best tandoori food in India. Most renowned is *raan* (leg of mutton), along with other meats, fish, and vegetables, each of which is marinated and grilled to succulent perfection in the traditional clay oven visible in the exhibition kitchen. Equally famous is *dal bukhara*, a creamy black lentil dish simmered overnight with tomatoes, ginger, and garlic and finished with homemade butter; it's become so popular it's now sold in grocery stores around town. Prices at this subcontinent stalwart have increased manifold since its inception, but our critics insist it's still the must-try for regional Indian cuisine in the capital city.

CRITICS' TIPS

Request to sit at a table with a sofa; it's far more comfortable than the wooden stool seating.

Be sure to order the "secret dish," chicken khurchan, *a more authentic take on the butter chicken found all over India. It's not on the menu but is always available upon request.*

Do as the locals do and eat with your hands. The staff encourages this and will loan you a cloth apron to keep your clothes from getting soiled.

ITC MAURYA HOTEL NEW DELHI
DIPLOMATIC ENCLAVE, SARDAR PATEL
MARG, NEW DELHI 110 021
+91 (11) 2611 2233
WWW.ITCHOTELS.IN/HOTELS/ITCMAURYA/
BUKHARA-RESTAURANT.ASPX

SOFT-SHELL CRAB WITH FLAME-ROASTED COCONUT

INDIA N ACCENT

[MODERN INDIAN] Tucked away in a boutique hotel that itself is tucked away in a tony Delhi residential enclave, Indian Accent is worthy of the effort it takes to find it. In a minimalist setting with accents of blonde wood and sleek granite, North India–born chef Manish Mehrotra offers adventurous and internationally influenced riffs on Indian street food that begs to be savored. Using his training in Southeast Asian cuisine, Chef Mehrotra mingles Asian flavors and inspirations from far corners of the globe into his dishes. Naan might arrive with melted Stilton. Chilean spareribs could be accented with dried mango. Foie gras–stuffed *galawat* with strawberry-chile chutney elevates and reinterprets curry in spectacular fashion. Another Mehrotra specialty—deep-fried soft-shell crab with spicy south Indian gunpowder masala and coconut (pictured at left)—won India's top TV food competition, *Foodistan*. The seven-course chef's tasting menu is the best way to experience Mehrotra's exciting, if not wild, Indian fusion. Some interesting wines are available, but even better are the cocktails—many with Indian flavors. Concocted by an inventive house mixologist, they are perfect accompaniments to a modern Indian dining experience.

CRITICS' TIPS

In good weather, ask for a table on the veranda.

Menus change seasonally and specialties daily. You will do well to let the chef choose dishes for you.

Tell your server what kind of food you like—French, Thai, Chinese, and so on—and the chef will design a menu that appeals to your palate.

THE MANOR
77 FRIENDS COLONY (WEST)
NEW DELHI 110065
+91 11 4323 5151
WWW.INDIANACCENT.COM

STIR-FRIED BANANA FLOWERS

KARAVALLI

[SOUTHWEST INDIAN] Karavalli is one of the first restaurants in India to serve the type of food enjoyed in the southwest coastal belt stretching across Goa, Mangalore, and Kerala. Presiding over the refined South Indian cuisine is Chef Naren Thimmaiah, who spent more than two decades collecting recipes from locals throughout the region. Amid environs resembling a traditionally tiled Mangalorean house, seafood is the star, with freshly caught baby lobster, squid, prawns, and ladyfish often among the offerings. Guests are invited to select from the day's catch and advise the chef of their preferred style of preparation, then he skillfully obliges, seasoning with spices ground that day. The abundance of local spices and fruits are best expressed in dishes such as Alleppy fish curry and *kori gassi*—chicken stewed in fragrant coconut gravy. *Attirachy ularthu*—a Kerala dish of lamb with onions, tomatoes, and spices—is tender, aromatic, and a worthy alternative to seafood. *Patrade*, or roasted, spiced lentils on *colocasia* leaves, showcases unusual and beguiling flavors and presentation.

CRITICS' TIPS

Request an outdoor table; in Bangalore's temperate climate, the leafy courtyard and its wrought-iron furniture beckon.

Order Kerala ghee rice and curry; it's a delicious mix of chicken curry and rice steamed in a banana leaf and topped with clarified butter.

As a contrast to the well-known North Indian naan *and* roti *flatbreads, try the rice-based* appams *and* dosas *served here.*

THE GATEWAY HOTEL, RESIDENCY ROAD
BANGALORE
66, RESIDENCY ROAD
BANGALORE
560 025, KARNATAKA
+91 80 6660 4545
WWW.THEGATEWAYHOTELS.COM/
RESIDENCYROADBANGALORE/RESTAURANTS.ASPX

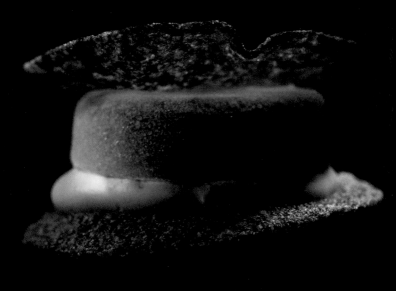

VIOLET POTATO CHIPS WITH POTATO ICE CREAM

IGGY'S

[MODERN EUROPEAN] Though born and bred in Singapore, globe-trotting sommelier Ignatius Chan is clearly a citizen of the world. His eponymous hometown restaurant provides a platform for the flavors and techniques he encountered during his exhaustive travels. Housed since late 2010 in the city's Orchard Road Hilton, the small dining room, with its chic, streamlined décor is an apt backdrop to Chef Akmal Anuar's adventurous food presented with modern European flair. While the dishes on the ever-changing tasting menu defy categorization, they tend to rely on French technique, choice seasonal ingredients from around the world—such as French foie gras, Welsh beef, Japanese *kurobuta* pork—and subtle influences from Southeast Asia and Japan. If you're lucky, the offerings will include *kurobuta* pork plated over onion confit and topped with a sunny-side up quail egg and white Alba truffle shavings. The unparalleled wine cellar owes as much to Chan's expertise as to his personal relationships with growers throughout the world. Heavily focused on Burgundy, Chan has said pinot noir is highly complementary to his inspired cuisine.

CRITICS' TIPS

Consider eating at the bar; the entrance and nearby dining counter are quite dramatic, and it's the only spot where you can select from the impressive à la carte menu.

Only a set menu is available in the dining room, but the staff will accommodate any dietary requests.

In the main dining room, don't miss the glass doors leading into the kitchen, which can be frosted over with the touch of a button.

THE HILTON HOTEL
581 ORCHARD ROAD, LEVEL 3
SINGAPORE 238883
+65 6732 2234
WWW.IGGYS.COM.SG

CONFIT OF PETUNA OCEAN TROUT WITH KELP, DAIKON, AND FENNEL

TETSUYA'S

[JAPANESE-INFLUENCED FRENCH] Run by Australia's most famous celebrity chef, Tetsuya Wakuda, this high-end Japanese-French restaurant in the center of Sydney is unparalleled in popularity. The serene dining room alone—with floor-to-ceiling windows overlooking a Japanese-inspired garden filled with bonsai trees and waterfalls—provides an urban oasis worthy of a visit. But the 10-course set tasting menu presided over by Tets, as the Japanese-born chef is often referred to, continues to be the main draw. Merging Japanese seasonal flavors and classic French technique, a meal here is likely to include Chef Wakuda's most famous dish, confit of ocean trout; on the menu for nearly 20 years and celebrated the world over, it's a melt-in-your-mouth combination of fish cooked *sous vide,* dredged in a dried kelp crust, served on shredded fennel, daikon, and shiso cress, and garnished with sake-marinated ocean trout roe. But throughout the hours-long meal, you may also be privy to chilled vegetable soup topped with yogurt ice cream or sashimi of kingfish—all expertly paired with a suggested wine from the restaurant's comprehensive list.

CRITICS' TIPS

Securing a seat requires reserving at least four weeks in advance.

Request a seat downstairs in one of three main rooms overlooking the gardens. The newer private dining areas upstairs lack the charm of the original room.

If you want to take some of Tetsuya's flavor home, buy the Tasmanian wasabi mustard or sliced smoked ocean trout, which are available through local retailers.

529 KENT STREET
SYDNEY NSW 2000
+61 2 9267 2900
WWW.TETSUYAS.COM

REGIONAL TOP 100
RESTAURANTS LISTS

Regional Top 100 Restaurants: France

PARIS

Le 21
Seafood
+33 (0)1 46 33 76 90

35 Degrés Ouest
French Seafood
+33 (0)1 42 86 98 88

**Les 110 de
Taillevent**
French Brasserie
+33 (0)1 40 74 20 20

Aida
Japanese
+33 (0)1 43 06 14 18

**Alain Ducasse au
Plaza Athénée**
French
+33 (0)1 53 67 65 00

L'Ambroisie
French
+33 (0)1 42 78 51 45

L'Arpège
Modern French
+33 (0)1 47 05 09 06

Restaurant Astier
Parisian Bistro
+33 (0)1 43 57 16 35

L'Astrance
Contemporary French
+33 (0)1 40 50 84 40

**L'Atelier de Joël
Robuchon L'Étoile**
French Gastronomic
+33 (0)1 47 23 75 75

**L'Atelier de
Joël Robuchon
Saint-Germain**
French
+33 (0)1 42 22 56 56

**Auberge Pyrénées
Cévennes**
Lyonnais and
Southwest French
+33 (0)1 43 57 33 78

L'Avant Comptoir
Classic French
+33 (0)1 41 01 01 01

Le Baratin
Modern French Bistro
+33 (0)1 43 49 39 70

Beef Club
French Bistro
+33 (0)9 54 37 13 65

Bistrot Paul Bert
French Bistro
+33 (0)1 43 72 24 01

Breizh Café
Breton Traditional
+33 (0)1 42 72 13 77

Carré des Feuillants
Modern French
+33 (0)1 42 86 82 82

Le Chateaubriand
Modern Bistro
+33 (0)1 43 57 45 95

Chez Georges
French Bistro
+33 (0)1 42 60 07 11

Chez René
French Bistro
+33 (0)1 43 54 30 23

**Les Cocottes de
Christian Constant**
Classic French
+33 (0)1 45 50 10 31

Le Comptoir du Relais
Southwest French
+33 (0)1 44 27 07 97

Le Coq Rico
Modern French
+33 (0)1 42 59 82 89

La Dame de Pic
Modern French
+33 (0)1 42 60 40 40

L'Entredgeu
French Bistro
+33 (0)1 40 54 97 24

Epicure
Modern French
+33 (0)1 53 43 43 40

Fish La Boissonnerie
Modern French
+33 (0)1 43 54 34 69

Fogón
Traditional Spanish
+33 (0)1 43 54 31 33

Frédéric Simonin
Modern French
+33 (0)1 45 74 74 74

Le Galopin
Gastronomic Bistro
+33 (0)1 42 06 05 03

Le Grand Véfour
French Gastronomic
+33 (0)1 42 96 56 27

Huitrerie Régis
Oyster Bar
+33 (0)1 44 41 10 07

Izakaya Issé
Japanese Sake Bistro
+33 (0)1 42 96 26 60

Jadis
French Bistro
+33 (0)1 45 57 73 20

Le Jeu de Quilles
French Bistro
+33 (0)1 53 90 76 22

Le Jules Verne
Contemporary French
+33 (0)1 45 55 61 44

Kotteri Ramen Naritake
Authentic Japanese Ramen
+33 (0)1 42 86 03 83

Laurent
Modern French
+33 (0)1 42 25 00 39

Michel Rostang
French Gastronomic
+33 (0)1 47 63 40 77

Neva Cuisine
Contemporary French Bistro
+33 (0)1 45 22 18 91

Passage 53
French Gastronomic
+33 (0)1 42 33 04 35

Pavillon Ledoyen
French Gastronomic
+33 (0)1 53 05 10 00

Philou
Classic French Bistro
+33 (0)1 42 38 00 13

Pierre Gagnaire
Modern French
+33 (0)1 58 36 12 50

Le Pré Catelan
Modern French
+33 (0)1 44 14 41 00

Racines
French Bistro
+33 (0)1 40 13 06 41

Restaurant Guy Savoy
French
+33 (0)1 43 80 40 61

Restaurant Hiramatsu
French Gastronomic
+33 (0)1 56 81 08 80

Restaurant Jean-François Piège
Modern French
+33 (0)1 47 05 49 75

Restaurant Le Meurice
Modern French
+33 (0)1 44 58 10 55

Restaurant Toyo
Japanese/French
+33 (0)1 43 54 28 03

Rino
Mediterranean
+33 (0)1 48 06 95 85

Roseval
Modern French
+33 (0)9 53 56 24 14

Saturne
Modern French
+33 (0)1 42 60 31 90

Semilla
Modern French
+33 (0)1 43 54 34 50

Septime
Modern French
+33 (0)1 43 67 38 29

Le Severo
Classic French
+33 (0)1 45 40 40 91

Shang Palace at the Shangri-La Hotel
Chinese
+33 (0)1 53 67 19 92

Le Sot l'y Laisse
French Bistro
+33 (0)1 40 09 79 20

Spring
Modern French
+33 (0)1 45 96 05 72

La Table d'Aki
Contemporary French
+33 (0)1 45 44 43 48

La Table d'Eugène
Modern French
+33 (0)1 42 55 61 64

La Table du Lancaster
Modern French
+33 (0)1 40 76 40 76

Taillevent
French
+33 (0)1 44 95 15 01

La Taverne de Zhao
Chinese
+33 (0)1 40 37 16 21

Au Trou Gascon
Southwest
Modern French
+33 (0)1 43 44 34 26

La Tute
French Bistro
+33 (0)1 40 15 65 65

Willi's Wine Bar
Modern Cuisine
+33 (0)1 42 61 05 09

yam'Tcha
French-Asian Fusion
+33 (0)1 40 26 08 07

Ze Kitchen Galerie
French-Asian Fusion
+33 (0)1 44 32 00 32

NORTH

BUSNES

Le Meurin
Regional Gastronomic
+33 (0)3 21 68 88 88

HONFLEUR

SaQuaNa
Gastronomic
+33 (0)2 31 89 40 80

LA MADELAINE-
SOUS-MONTREUIL

La Grenouillère
Contemporary French
+33 (0)3 21 06 07 22

REIMS

Le Parc at Château Les Crayéres
French Gastronomic
+33 (0)3 26 24 90 00

EAST

MEGÈVE

Flocons de Sel
Contemporary French
+33 (0)4 50 21 49 99

CENTRAL

CHAGNY

Lameloise
Neoclassical
+33 (0)3 85 87 65 65

LINDRY

Les Grès
Modern Bistro
+33 (0)9 52 31 64 10

SAULIEU

Relais Bernard Loiseau
French Gastronomic
+33 (0)3 80 90 53 53

ROANNE

Maison Troisgros
Modern French
+33 (0)4 77 71 66 97

COLLONGES-
AU-MONT-D'OR

L'Auberge du Pont de Collonges
Gastronomic
+33 (0)4 72 42 90 90

LYON

La Mère Brazier
Neoclassical
+33 (0)4 78 23 17 20

SAINT-BONNET
-LE-FROID

Régis et Jacques Marcon
Modern French
+33 (0)4 71 59 93 72

CHAUDES-AIGUES

Serge Vieira
Gastronomic
+33 (0)4 71 20 73 85

VALENCE

Pic
French Gastronomic
+33 (0)4 75 44 15 32

SOUTH

FONTJONCOUSE

Auberge du Vieux Puits
French
+33 (0)4 68 44 07 37

LASTOURS

Le Puits du Trésor
Seasonal French
+33 (0)4 68 77 50 24

LAGUIOLE

Bras
Modern French
+33 (0)5 65 51 18 20

LORMONT

Restaurant Jean-Marie Amat
Gastronomic
+33 (0)5 56 06 12 52

SAINT-PÉE-SUR-NIVELLE

L'Auberge Basque
Neoclassical
+33 (0)5 59 51 70 00

PROVENCE-ALPES-CÔTE D'AZUR

MONDRAGON

Restaurant La Beaugravière
Traditional Regional
+33 (0)4 90 40 82 54

GIGONDAS

L'Oustalet
Gastronomic
+33 (0)4 90 65 85 30

AVIGNON

La Mirande
Gastronomic
+33 (0)4 90 14 20 20

ARLES

La Chassagnette
Organic Gastronomic
+33 (0)4 90 97 26 96

VENCE

Le Saint Martin
Gastronomic Provençal
+33 (0)4 93 58 02 02

JUAN-LES-PINS

La Passagère
Gastronomic
+33 (0)4 93 61 02 79

ÈZE

Château Eza
French and Mediterranean
+33 (0)4 93 41 12 24

La Chèvre d'Or
Gastronomic
+33 (0)4 92 10 66 66

MENTON

Mirazur
Modern Mediterranean
+33 (0)4 92 41 86 86

MONACO

Le Louis XV
Modern Gastronomic French
+377 98 06 88 64

Regional Top 100 Restaurants: Japan

TOKYO

Akasaka Kikunoi
Japanese Kaiseki
+81 3 3568 6055

Apicius
Authentic French
+81 3 3214 1361

Banraien
Chinese
+81 3 3450 5667

Baron Okura
French and Chinese
+81 3 3224 7109

Chugoku Hanten Fureika
Chinese
+81 3 5561 7788

Ebisu Kuroiwa
Japanese Kappo
+81 3 5793 9618

Edo-Soba Hosokawa
Japanese Soba Noodle
+81 3 3626 1125

L'Effervescence
French Gastronomy
+81 3 5766 9500

Esquisse
Modern French
+81 3 5537 5580

Fukurinmon
Cantonese
+81 3 6215 6996

Gentoushi Nakada
Japanese
+81 90 4228 3817

Halekai's
World Fusion Cuisine
+81 3 3560 8012

Horikane
Japanese
+81 3 3280 4629

Ishikawa
Japanese Kaiseki
+81 3 5225 0173

Iyuki
Japanese
+81 3 5550 2022

Kadowaki
Japanese Kappo
+81 3 5772 2553

Kanda
Japanese Kaiseki
+81 3 5786 0150

Kanesada
Japanese Sushi
+81 3 3403 3648

Kawamura
Japanese Steakhouse
+81 3 3289 8222

Kitcho Tokyo
Japanese Kaiseki
+81 3 3541 8228

Kohaku
Japanese Kaiseki
+81 3 5225 0807

Kozasa
Japanese Sushi
+81 3 5458 2828

Kun
Fusion
+81 3 5570 4117

Kurogi
Japanese Kaiseki
+81 3 5846 3510

Kyo Aji
Japanese
+81 3 3591 3344

Lauburu
French Bistro
+81 3 3498 1314

Makino
Fugu/Blowfish Hot Pot
+81 3 3844 6659

Mikawa Zezankyo
Japanese Tempura
+81 3 3643 8383

Musashi
Japanese Sushi
+81 3 5464 3634

Nodaiwa
Traditional Unagi/Eel
+81 3 3583 7852

Ogino
French
+81 3 5481 1333

Okina
Soba/Japanese Kaiseki
+81 3 3477 2648

Ozaki
Japanese Sushi/ Kappo
+81 3 3454 1682

Raisan
Japanese Kaiseki
+81 3 6416 8474

Rakutei
Japanese Tempura
+81 3 3585 3743

**Restaurant
Quintessence**
Modern French
+81 3 5791 3715

Ristorante ASO
Italian
+81 3 3770 3690

RyuGin
Japanese
+81 3 3423 8006

Ryutenmon
Cantonese
+81 3 5423 7865

Sawada
Japanese Sushi
+81 3 3571 4711

Shigeyoshi
Japanese Kappo
+81 3 3400 4044

Sukiyabashi Jiro
Japanese Sushi
+81 3 3535 3600

Sushi Nakamura
Japanese Sushi
+81 3 3746 0856

Sushi Saito
Japanese Sushi
+81 3 3589 4412

Sushi Shin
Japanese Sushi
+81 3 5485 0031

Sushi Sho
Japanese Sushi
+81 3 3351 6387

Sushi Tsubaki
Japanese Sushi
+81 3 3572 7807

Sushiso Masa
Japanese
+81 3 3499 9178

Takazawa
Modern Japanese
+81 3 3505 5052

Tarantella da Luigi
Italian
+81 3 6408 5552

Il Teatrino Da Salone
Italian
+81 3 3400 5077

Tomura
Kyoto/Japanese Kaiseki
+81 3 3591 3303

Wakiya Ichiemicharou
Modern Chinese
+81 3 5574 8861

Yamashita
European/Continental
+81 3 6413 1144

Yukimura
Japanese
+81 3 5772 1610

KYOTO

Chihana
Japanese Kappo
+81 75 561 2741

Gion Maruyama
Japanese Kaiseki
+81 75 525 0009

Gion Sasaki
Japanese Kaiseki
+81 75 551 5000

Hamasaku
Japanese
+81 75 561 0330

Hayashi
Kyoto Cuisine
+81 75 213 4409

Ichihan
Japanese Sushi
+81 6 6641 2437

Kappo Masuda
Japanese Kappo
+81 75 361 1508

Kichisen
Kaiseki
+81 75 711 6121

Kikunoi Honten
Japanese Kaiseki
+81 75 561 0015

Kinmata
Japanese Kaiseki
+81 75 221 1039

Kitcho Arashiyama
Japanese Kaiseki
+81 75 881 1101

Kodaiji Wakuden
Japanese
+81 75 533 3100

Mishimatei
Sukiyaki
+81 75 221 0003

Misoguigawa
French Kaiseki
+81 75 221 2270

Miyamasou
Japanese Kaiseki
+81 75 746 0231

Mizai
Japanese Kaiseki
+81 75 551 3310

**Nishimura Kyoto
(Kyo-Ryori Nishimura)**
Kyoto Cuisine
+81 75 241 0070

Sakurada
Japanese Kaiseki
+81 75 371 2552

Shingo
Steakhouse
+81 75 551 2253

Shuhaku
Japanese
+81 75 551 2711

Sojiki Nakahigashi
Japanese
+81 75 752 3500

Tawaraya Ryokan
Ryokan/Japanese
Kaiseki
+81 75 211 5566

Uozuya
Japanese
+81 75 312 2538

HOKKAIDO/
SAPPORO

Sushi Tanabe
Japanese Sushi
+81 11 520 2202

NAGANO

**Fogliolina della Porta
Fortuna**
Italian
+81 267 41 0612

Yukawatan
French Gastronomy
+81 267 46 6200

KANAGAWA/
HAKONE

Gôra Kadan
Japanese Kaiseki
+81 460 82 3331

SHIZUOKA

Asaba
Japanese Kaiseki/
Ryokan
+81 558 72 7000

KANAZAWA

Ryokan Asadaya
Kaiseki-Ryōri
+81 76 231 2228

FUKUI

Etizen Mikuni Kawaki
Japanese Crab
+81 776 82 1313

GIFU

Kaikatei
Chinese
+81 582 64 5811

OSAKA

Hajime
Modern French
+81 6 6447 6688

Kahala
Japanese Fusion
+81 6 6345 6778

Kakoiyama
Japanese Nabe
+81 6 6341 1168

Kigawa Asai
Japanese
+81 6 6243 7100

KOBE

Kobe Aragawa
Steakhouse
+81 78 221 8547

NARA

Akordu
Modern Spanish
+81 742 43 0222

SHIGA

Shofukurou
Japanese Kaiseki
+81 748 22 0003

MIE

Wadakin
Sukiyaki
+81 598 21 1188

TOTTORI

Kaniyoshi
Japanese Crab
+81 857 22 7738

TOKUSHIMA

Kokin Aoyagi
Japanese
+81 88 688 1155

FUKUOKA

Ebisudo
Japanese Kappo
+81 92 282 4825

Sushi Asou Hirao Sansou
Japanese Sushi
+81 92 524 5777

OITA

Yufuin Tamanoyu
Onsen Ryokan/
Japanese
+81 977 84 2158

MIYAZAKI

Issin Sushi Koyo
Japanese Sushi
+81 985 60 5005

Regional Top 100 Restaurants: The United States

NEW YORK AREA

15 East
Japanese Kaiseki/Sushi
212.647.0015

ABC Kitchen
American
212.475.5829

Annisa
Creative American
212.741.6699

Aureole
Progressive American
212.319.1660

Le Bernardin
French Seafood
212.554.1515

Blanca
Italian
347.799.2807

Blue Hill at Stone Barns
Seasonal American
914.366.9600

Bouley
French
212.964.2525

Brushstroke
Japanese
212.791.3771

Café Boulud
French American
212.772.2600

Chef's Table at Brooklyn Fare
Modern Japanese
718.243.0050

Corton
Modern French
212.219.2777

Daniel
French
212.288.0033

Degustation
Spanish
212.979.1012

Del Posto
Italian
212.497.8090

Donguri
Japanese
212.737.5656

Empellón Cocina
Progressive Mexican
212.780.0999

Fatty Crab
Malaysian Inspired
212.352.3592

Gotham Bar & Grill
Modern American
212.620.4020

Gramercy Tavern
American Seasonal
212.477.0777

La Grenouille
French
212.752.1495

Hakubai
Japanese Kaiseki
212.885.7111

Ichimura at Brushstroke
Japanese Kaiseki/
Edo-Mae Sushi
212.791.3771

Jean-Georges
French
212.299.3900

Junoon
Modern Indian
212.490.2100

Kajitsu
Japanese Shōjin
212.228.4873

Kurumazushi
Japanese
212.317.2802

Kyo Ya
Japanese
212.982.4140

Marea
Coastal Italian
212.582.5100

Masa
Japanese
212.823.9800

The Modern
French Alsatian
212.333.1220

Momofuku Ko
New American/
Contemporary
(no phone number)

Morimoto
Contemporary
Japanese
212.989.8883

Nobu
Modern Japanese
212.219.0500

The North Fork Table & Inn
Progressive American
631.765.0177

Per Se
Contemporary American
212.823.9335

Peter Luger Steakhouse
Steakhouse
718.387.7400

Rosanjin
Japanese Kaiseki
212.346.0664

Soto
Contemporary Japanese
212.414.3088

Sugiyama
Japanese Kaiseki
212.956.0670

Sushi Azabu
Japanese Sushi
212.274.0428

Sushi of Gari
Japanese Sushi
212.517.5340

Sushi Seki
Japanese Sushi
212.371.0238

Sushi Yasuda
Japanese Sushi
212.972.1001

Torrisi Italian Specialties Restaurant
Italian-American
212.965.0955

Tsukushi
Japanese Sushi
212.599.8888

Veritas
Contemporary American
212.353.3700

WD-50
Modern American
212.477.2900

EAST

BOSTON AREA

Cala's Restaurant
New American
978.525.3304

Menton
French-Italian
617.737.0099

O Ya
Modern Japanese
617.654.9900

Uni Sashimi Bar
Contemporary Japanese Sashimi
617.536.7200

PHILADELPHIA, PA

Vetri
Northern Italian
215.732.3478

WASHINGTON, DC

Minibar by José Andrés
Avant-Garde
202.393.0812

SOUTHEAST

WASHINGTON, VA

Inn at Little Washington
Refined American
540.675.3800

CHARLESTON, SC

McCrady's
Regional American
843.577.0025

WALLAND, TN

Blackberry Farm
Regional American
865.984.8166

BIRMINGHAM, AL

Highlands Bar & Grill
French-Inspired Regional American
205.939.1400

MIDWEST

CHICAGO, IL

Alinea
Modernist
312.867.0110

L2O
Modern Seafood
773.868.0002

TRU
Progressive French
312.202.0001

SOUTHWEST

AUSTIN, TX

Uchiko
Japanese Farmhouse
512.916.4808

LAS VEGAS, NV

**Bartolotta Ristorante
di Mare**
Italian Seafood
702.770.3305

Joël Robuchon
French
702.891.7925

Restaurant Guy Savoy
Contemporary French
702.731.7110

**Twist by Pierre
Gagnaire**
French
888.881.9367

NORTHWEST

WOODINVILLE, WA

The Herbfarm
Pacific Northwestern
425.485.5300

WEST

SAN FRANCISCO BAY
AREA

Acquerello
Contemporary Italian
415.567.5432

Atelier Crenn
Modern French
415.440.0460

Auberge du Soleil
French Mediterranean
707.963.1211

Baumé
Modern French
650.328.8899

Benu
Contemporary
American
415.685.4860

Chez Panisse
California
510.548.5525

Coi
Contemporary
California
415.393.9000

Commis
Northern California
510.653.3902

Frances
Modern California
415.621.3870

The French Laundry
Contemporary
American
707.944.2380

Keiko à Nob Hill
French-California with
Japanese Influences
415.829.7141

Manresa
California
408.354.4330

Michael Mina
Modern American
415.397.9222

Mitsunobu
Contemporary
Japanese
650.234.1084

**The Restaurant
at Meadowood**
Modern American
707.967.1205

RN74
Contemporary French
415.543.7474

State Bird Provisions
New American
415.795.1272

Sushi Sam's Edomata
Japanese Sushi
650.344.0888

Terra
Seasonal New American
707.963.8931

The Village Pub
Contemporary
American
650.851.9888

Wakuriya
Japanese Kaiseki
650.286.0410

PASO ROBLES, CA

Bistro Laurent
French Bistro
805.226.8191

LOS ANGELES AREA

**The Bazaar By
José Andrés**
Modern Spanish
310.246.5555

Matsuhisa
Modern Japanese
310.659.9639

Mélisse
French-American
310.395.0881

Nishimura LA
Japanese/Sushi
310.659.4770

Pizzeria Mozza
Italian
323.297.0101

Providence
Modern American
Seafood
323.460.4170

Urasawa
Sushi
310.247.8939

**Wolfgang Puck
at Hotel Bel-Air**
Modern Californian
310.909.1644

SAN DIEGO, CA

Addison
Contemporary French
858.314.1900

HONOLULU, HI

Chef Mavro
Contemporary Eurasian
808.944.4714

Hiroshi Eurasian Tapas
Eurasian
808.533.4476

UNITED KINGDOM

LONDON

Alain Ducasse at the Dorchester
Contemporary French
+44 20 7629 8866

Alyn Williams at the Westbury
Modern European
+44 20 7078 9579

Amaya
Modern Indian Grill
+44 20 7823 1166

Café Spice Namasté
Pan-Indian
+44 20 7488 9242

Cinnamon Club
Modern Indian
+44 20 7222 2555

Dinner by Heston Blumenthal
Contemporary British
+44 20 7201 3833

Le Gavroche
French
+44 20 7408 0881

The Greenhouse
French
+44 20 7499 3331

Hakkasan
Modern Chinese
+44 20 7927 7000

Hibiscus
Contemporary French
+44 20 7629 2999

Koffmann's
Provincial French
+44 20 7107 8844

The Ledbury
Modern British
+44 20 7792 9090

Locanda Locatelli
Italian
+44 20 7935 9088

Medlar
French Inspired
+44 20 7349 1900

Nobu London
Contemporary Japanese
+44 20 7447 4747

One-O-One
Contemporary Seafood
+44 20 7290 7101

Quilon
Contemporary Southwest Coastal Indian
+44 20 7821 1899

Rasoi
Southwest Coastal Indian
+44 20 7225 1881

Restaurant Gordon Ramsay
Modern French
+44 20 7352 4441

The Square
French
+44 20 7495 7100

St. John
British
+44 20 3301 8069

Umu
Contemporary Japanese
+44 20 7499 8881

The Wolseley
European
+44 20 7499 6996

BRAY

The Fat Duck
Modern British
+44 1628 580 333

The Waterside Inn
French
+44 1628 620 691

OXFORD

Le Manoir aux Quat'Saisons
Modern French
+44 184 427 8881

WANDSWORTH COMMON

Chez Bruce
Modern Regional French & Mediterranean
+44 20 8672 0114

CHELTENHAM

Le Champignon Sauvage
Modern Seasonal French
+44 12 4257 3449

ABERGAVENNY

The Walnut Tree
International
+44 18 7385 2797

SWEDEN

STOCKHOLM

Frantzén/Lindeberg
Nordic
+46 8 20 85 80

DENMARK

COPENHAGEN

Noma
Local/Seasonal
+45 3296 3297

BELGIUM

BRUSSELS

Neptune
Modern French
+32 489 30 33 50

BRUGES

De Karmeliet
Modern Flemish
+32 50 33 82 59

Hertog Jan
Modern European
+32 50 67 34 46

DE PANNE

Hostellerie le Fox
Modern Belgian
+32 58 41 28 55

DRANOUTER

In De Wulf
Modern Flemish
+32 57 44 55 67

NETHERLANDS

ROTTERDAM

Parkheuvel
Modern French
+31 10 43 60 530

GERMANY

WOLFSBURG

Aqua
Contemporary German
+49 5361 606056

TRAVEMÜNDE

La Belle Epoque
Refined Avant-Garde
+49 4502 3080

AUSTRIA

VIENNA

Steirereck
Contemporary Austrian
+43 1 713 31 68

SWITZERLAND

CRISSIER

Restaurant de l'Hôtel de Ville
French
+41 21 634 05 05

ITALY

MILAN

Il Luogo di Aimo e Nadia
Creative Italian
+39 02 416886

BRUSAPORTO

Da Vittorio
Creative Lombardy
+39 035 681024

NOVARA

Al Sorriso
Regional Italian
+39 03 2298 3228

Villa Crespi
Contemporary Mediterranean
+39 0322 911902

MANTOVA

Ristorante dal Pescatore
Modern Italian
+39 03 7672 3001

MODENA

Osteria Francescana
Modern Italian
+39 059 210118

RUBANO

Le Calandre
Italian
+39 049 633000

VENICE

Harry's Bar
Italian
+39 041 528 5777

Osteria Alle Testiere
Italian Seafood
+39 041 522 7220

**Osteria Enoteca
San Marco**
Modern Italian
+39 041 528 5242

Ristorante "da Ivo"
Venetian
+39 041 528 5004

PORTOFINO

Da Puny
Genovese
+39 0185 26 9037

FORTE DEI MARMI

Ristorante Lorenzo
Italian Seafood
+39 0584 89671

NAPLES

Don Alfonso 1890
Modern Mediterranean
+39 081 878 00 26

SPAIN

SAN SEBASTIAN

Akelarre
Innovative Basque
l 34 943 31 12 09

Arzak
Innovative Basque
+34 943 27 84 65

ERRENTERIA

Mugaritz
Creative
+34 943 522 455

ATXONDO, BIZKAIA

Asador Etxebarri
Traditional Basque
+34 946 58 30 42

GIPUZKOA

Martín Berasategui
Contemporary Basque
+34 943 366 471

BARCELONA

Can Fabes
Modern Catalan
+34 938 67 28 51

SANTO POL DE MAR

Restaurant Sant Pau
Internationally
Influenced Spanish
+ 34 937 60 06 62

GIRONA

El Celler de Can Roca
Modern Spanish
+34 972 222 157

PORTUGAL

LISBON

Belcanto
Avant-Garde Portugese
+351 21 342 06 07

CHINA

BEIJING

**Family Li
Imperial Cuisine**
Chinese
+86 10 66180107

HONG KONG

Bo Innovation
Modern Chinese
+852 2850 8371

Fook Lam Moon
Cantonese
+852 2866 0663

Lung King Heen
Cantonese
+852 3196 8880

One Harbour Road
Cantonese
+852 2584 7722

Sun Tung Lok
Cantonese
+852 2152 1417

Yung Kee
Cantonese
+852 2522 1624

MACAU

Robuchon au Dôme
Modern French
+853 8803 7878

THAILAND

BANGKOK

Krua Apsorn
Traditional Thai
+66 2 668 8788

Mezzaluna
Modern International
+66 2 624 9555

Nahm
Thai
+66 2 625 3388

BALI

UBUD

Ibu Oka
Indonesian
+62 361 97 64 35

Mozaic
Contemporary French-
Indonesian
+62 361 975768

PHILIPPINES

TAGAYTAY

Antonio's
European-Asian Fusion
+63 917 899 2866

INDIA

NEW DELHI

Bukhara
Northwest Frontier
Indian
+91 11 26112233

Dum Pukht
Indian
+91 11 26112233

Indian Accent
Modern Indian
+91 11 43235151

Varq
Contemporary Indian
+91 11 23 02 61 62

MUMBAI

Gajalee
Malvani & Konkani
Seafood
+91 22 26 16 64 70

The Thai Pavilion
Contemporary Thai
+91 22 66 65 08 08

GOA

Beach House
Goan-Portuguese
Fusion
+91 832 664 5555

CHENNAI

Southern Spice
South Indian
+91 44 66 00 28 27

BANGALORE

Karavalli
Southwest Indian
+91 80 66604545

SINGAPORE

**Crystal Jade Golden
Palace**
Contemporary
Cantonese/Teochew
Fine Dining
+65 6734 6866

Iggy's
Modern European
+65 6732 2234

**Imperial Treasure
Teochew Cuisine**
Teochew & Cantonese
+65 6736 2118

Jaan
French
+65 9199 9008

My Humble House
Contemporary Chinese
+65 6423 1881

**Taste Paradise
Restaurant**
Contemporary Chinese
+65 6509 9660

AUSTRALIA

SYDNEY

Buon Ricordo
Italian
+61 2 9360 6729

Marque
Contemporary French
+61 2 9332 2225

Quay
Modern Australian
+61 2 9251 5600

Rockpool Bar & Grill
Modern Australian
+61 2 8078 1900

Tetsuya's
Japanese-Influenced
French
+61 2 9267 2900

BRISBANE

Esquire
Seasonal International
Grill
+61 7 3220 2123

MELBOURNE

Vue de Monde
Modern Australian
+61 3 9691 3888

Contributing Critics and Foodie Editors

SAMIR ARORA

Samir Arora is the publisher and editor of the Foodie guides and the founder and CEO of Glam Media. He grew up in a multigenerational family food and restaurant business before joining Apple Computer in the 1980s and ultimately founding and investing in several Silicon Valley start-ups. He lived in Paris for three years and has studied *cha-kaiseki* and Zen *shōjin-ryōri* cuisine in Kyoto. He now divides his time between Woodside, California, and New York City, and he likes to spend his weekends planting, growing, sampling, cooking, and tasting food.

PATRICIA WELLS

Born in America and residing in Paris since 1980, multiple James Beard Award–winner Patricia Wells was the global restaurant critic for the *International Herald Tribune* for nearly 30 years as well as a restaurant critic for *L'Express Paris* and food writer and editor for the *New York Times*. The author of 14 widely heralded cookbooks and food books, she is also the founder of At Home with Patricia Wells, a cooking school that attracts food lovers from around the world to her kitchens in Paris and Provence. *www.patriciawells.com*

GAEL GREENE

American-born Gael Greene has been a restaurant critic and columnist for 44 years—40 of them as the Insatiable Critic for *New York* magazine, where she changed the way New Yorkers think and talk about food. The Manhattan resident also cofounded Citymeals-on-Wheels with famed American chef and food writer James Beard in 1981 to help feed New York's homebound elderly. The author of seven books, including *Everything You Always Wanted to Know about Ice Cream but Were*

Too Fat to Ask, The Mafia Guide to Dining Out, Nobody Knows the Truffles I've Seen, and her recent memoir *Insatiable: Tales from a Life of Delicious Excess,* Gael is currently the restaurant critic for *Manhattan* magazine, an editorial consultant and writer for Glam Media, and the author of a weekly restaurant blog, BITE, and the newsletter *ForkPlay. www.insatiable-critic.com*

MASUHIRO YAMAMOTO

Best known in the United States for his commentary in the documentary film *Jiro Dreams of Sushi,* Tokyo-born food critic Masuhiro Yamamoto has been writing about restaurants since 1973 with a primary focus on Japan and Europe. He has authored guides to Tokyo restaurants, is the recipient of the French government's Ordre du Mérite Agricole for his contributions promoting French cuisine, and he has also penned books on opera and sports. Today he is still one of Japan's best-known and trusted culinary voices and is involved in a variety of projects, ranging from special events to television to food-product development.

RUTH REICHL

The editor in chief of *Gourmet* magazine from 1999 to 2009, American journalist and author Ruth Reichl began writing about food in 1972 and launched her career as a restaurant critic with *New West* and *California* magazines. She went on to become the restaurant critic and food editor of the *Los Angeles Times* from 1984 to 1993 and the restaurant critic for the *New York Times* from 1993 to 1999. Ruth has authored four memoirs and today is the editor of *The Modern Library Food Series* books and is executive producer and host of the public television series *Adventures with Ruth.* She is also a producer on the upcoming movie based on her book *Garlic and Sapphires* and is working on a novel, a cookbook, and a memoir. *www.ruthreichl.com / Twitter: @ruthreichl*

JONATHAN GOLD

The first food critic to win the Pulitzer Prize, Los Angeles–based Jonathan Gold began his food-writing career at *LA Weekly* in 1986, with his "Counter Intelligence" column, which explored Los Angeles's often-unreported ethnic neighborhoods and their restaurants. He took the column to the *Los Angeles Times* from 1990 to 1996 and penned destination-restaurant reviews for *California* and *Los Angeles* magazines before becoming *Gourmet* magazine's New York restaurant critic and publishing *Counter Intelligence: Where to Eat in the Real Los Angeles*. Jonathan is the restaurant critic for the *Los Angeles Times*.

BRUNO VERJUS

A native of Roanne, France, Paris-based journalist Bruno Verjus has been writing about food for a decade. The author of several cookbooks, he currently contributes to French publications *Omnivore*, *T3ois Couleurs*, and *France Culture* and is a gastronomy expert for the Paris auction house Artcurial. His blog, Food Intelligence, which was founded in 2005, is considered one of France's most influential online commentaries of French gastronomy. *www.foodintelligence.blogspot.com*

ALEXANDER LOBRANO

American-born James Beard award–winning journalist Alexander Lobrano grew up in Connecticut and resided in Boston, New York, and London before moving to his current residence, Paris, France, in 1986. The European correspondent for *Gourmet* magazine for 10 years, he has written about food and travel for *Bon Appétit*, *Food & Wine*, *Travel & Leisure*, *Departures*, *Condé Nast Traveler*, and other American publications, and he is the author of *Hungry for Paris: The Ultimate Guide to the City's 102*

Best Restaurants. Ongoing assignments with *Saveur* and the *New York Times* ensure Alec sleuths out the best restaurants from the farthest corners of the globe. *Alexanderlobrano.com*

CHARLES CAMPION

A chef and award-winning journalist, U.K.-based Charles Campion wrote about food and restaurants for the *London Evening Standard* for nearly 20 years. He also worked for *The Independent, The Times, The Weekend Telegraph*, and a host of other magazines. Currently he's a judge on the BBC TV shows *MasterChef* and *Professional MasterChef*, and he is the author of multiple food and cookery books, including *Charles Campion's Guide to London Restaurants*, which is in its tenth edition. He lives near Worcester and is an adviser to Slow Food U.K. and a patron of Oxford Brookes University. *www.charlescampion.com*

VIR SANGHVI

London-born Vir Sanghvi is the best-known Indian journalist of his generation. A print and television journalist, columnist, and talk show host, he was the youngest editor in the history of Indian journalism when he was appointed editor of *Bombay* magazine at the age of 22. He went on to grow India's *Sunday* magazine into the country's largest-selling English-language news magazine and spent eight years overseeing *Hindustan Times*, the largest-selling English-language newspaper in Delhi and North India. The author of *Hindustan Times's* hugely popular "Rude Food" column, Vir was bestowed the Best Food Critic award from the Indian Culinary Foundation. Vir is the creator and host of highly successful Southeast Asian food television shows *A Matter of Taste* and *Vir Sanghvi's Asian Diary.*

AUN KOH

Singapore native Aun Koh is the publisher and cofounder of *The Miele Guide*, the independent Asia regional survey that annually profiles the continent's 500 best restaurants. A cofounder of the Ate Group, an award-winning Singapore-based integrated communications agency, Aun started his media career with the *International Herald Tribune* and *Newsweek*, in Paris and New York respectively, before relocating to Hong Kong and ultimately his hometown. In 1998, Aun launched *East* magazine, then Asia's first regional lifestyle magazine. A die-hard foodie, Aun also coauthored three cookbooks and in 2005 helped launch Chubby Hubby, one of the world's most popular food and travel websites. *Twitter: @aunkoh*

SUSUMU OHTA

Tokyo-born president and publisher of Ohta Publications Co. Ltd., Susumu "Sam" Ohta was raised around the hospitality industry, and by age 15 he was apprenticing in fine hotels and restaurants throughout the United States, Switzerland, and Japan. After graduating from the Culinary Institute of America in New York, Susumu joined Ohta Publications, a publishing company operated by his father. As president, he dines out 200 days each year and oversees culinary articles and sales promotion activities across 35 countries around the world. In addition to his publishing business, he provides support and consultation services for overseas hotels and restaurants planning to open in the Japanese market or looking for quality human resources within the hospitality industry. *Ohtapub.co.jp*

KUNDO KOYAMA

Born in Kumamoto, Japan, Kundo Koyama is a Tokyo-based screenwriter, scriptwriter, and novelist who garnered an International Emmy Award for conceptualizing and writing

Iron Chef, the Japanese television show and chefs' competition that launched in 1993 and inspired the equally popular U.S. spin-off. He also earned the Best Script award at the Japan Academy Awards and the Best Foreign Language Film award at the U.S. Academy Awards for his screenplay *Departures*. Currently, he is engaged in the production of the recent resurrection of Japan's *Iron Chef* and a new TV show, *Kundo Koyama's Tokyo Meeting*.

YUKI YAMAMURA

The chief executive officer of Glam Media Japan and former CEO of DoubleClick Japan and Excite Japan, Yuki Yamamura is one of Japan's top digital media industry pioneers. A Tokyo resident for the past 20 years, he is also one of the top Japanese food and wine bloggers, having authored more than a thousand articles about restaurants, food, and wine in his country and abroad. *Brash.glam.jp/yuki*

ERIKA LENKERT

Foodie Top 100 Restaurants Managing Executive editor Erika Lenkert is a San Francisco–based media veteran with 20 years of industry experience writing for lifestyle publications such as *Food Network*, *Everyday with Rachel Ray*, *Travel & Leisure*, and *Food & Wine*. She has held restaurant columns in *San Francisco* and *Los Angeles* magazines, was a food critic for the *San Francisco Chronicle*, and has authored several books, including *The Last-Minute Party Girl*, *Healthy Eating During Pregnancy*, *Frommer's San Francisco*, and *Frommer's Wine Country*. The coauthor of the groundbreaking *Raw: The Uncook Book*, she has also managed and edited a variety of print and online media projects.

Index

Photo Credits

Page 6, photo © Dino Baranzelli.
Page 16, photos © Pierre Monetta (all).
Page 18, photos © Owen Franken (all).
Page 20, photos © Bernhard Winkelmann (bottom left), © Philippe Vaures-Santamaria (bottom right), © DosSantos/Lemone (main).
Page 22, photos courtesy of L'Astrance (bottom left and right), © Richard Haughton (main). **Page 24,** photos © David Arous/Degresfahrenheit.com (all). **Page 27,** photo © Michael Paul/StockFood Creative/Getty Images. **Page 28,** photos courtesy of Carré des Feuillants (all). **Page 30,** photos © Patricia Grunler-Westermann (all).
Page 32, photos © Michael Roulier (bottom left), © Elisabeth Lhomelet (main), © François Goizé (bottom right).
Page 34, photos © Roméo Balancourt (bottom right), © Jean-Baptiste Leroux (bottom left), © Philippe Barret (main).
Page 36, photos © David Grimbert-Les Ateliers Apicius (main and bottom right), © Thai Toutain (bottom left). **Page 38,** photos © Jacques Gavard (all). **Page 40,** photos © FRANCK PRIGNET/Le Figaro Magazine (bottom right), © FRANCOIS GUENET/TV Magazine (main and bottom left).
Page 42, photos © Stevens Fremont (bottom left), © Brian Leatart (bottom right), © Laurence Mouton (main). **Page 44,** photos © Stéphane de Bourgies (all).
Page 46, photos © Alexandra Meurant (all).
Page 48, photo © Zoonar/Thinkstock.
Page 50, photos © Alexandra Meurant (all).
Page 52, photos courtesy of Shangri-La Hotel, Paris (all). **Page 54,** photos © Lucien Lung/Le Figaro (bottom left and right), © Vincent Delmas/Critique-gastronomique.com (main). **Page 56,** photos © Ihibaut Ruggeri (all). **Page 58,** photos © Hai-Er Zhang (bottom right), © Francesco Acerbis (main), © Chi Wah Chan (bottom left).
Page 60, photos © Eric Laignel (all).
Page 62, photos © Marie-Pierre Morel (bottom left), © Laurent Boton (main), © Cyrille Weiner (bottom right).
Page 64, photos courtesy of Flocons de Sel (all). **Page 66,** photos © Marie-Pierre Morel (all). **Page 68,** photos © Nami-Nami.blogspot.com (all). **Page 71,** photo © iStockphoto/Thinkstock. **Page 72,** photos © Fabrice Charrondiere (all). **Page 74,** photos © Alexandre Lardeur (all).

Page 76, photos © Pierre-François Couderc (main and bottom left), © Per-Anders Jorgensen (bottom right). **Page 78,** photos © Thomas Dhellemmes (main and bottom left), © Bernard Touillon (bottom right).
Page 82, photos © Satoshi Osaki (all).
Page 84, photos © Satoshi Osaki (all).
Page 86, photos © Satoshi Osaki (all).
Page 88, photos © Satoshi Osaki (all).
Page 90, photos © Satoshi Osaki (all).
Page 92, photos © Satoshi Osaki (all).
Page 96, photos © Satoshi Osaki (all).
Page 98, photos © Satoshi Osaki (all).
Page 100, photos © Satoshi Osaki (all).
Page 102, photos © Seiji Yamamoto (all).
Page 104, photos © Kenji Miura (all).
Page 106, photos © Satoshi Osaki (all).
Page 108, photos © Satoshi Osaki (all).
Page 110, photos © Satoshi Osaki (all).
Page 112, photos © Kazuyoshi Miyoshi (bottom left), courtesy of Gôra Kadan (main and bottom right). **Page 114,** photos © Satoshi Osaki (all). **Page 116,** photos courtesy of Hamasaku.co (all).
Page 118, photos © Satoshi Osaki (all).
Page 120, photos © Satoshi Osaki (main and bottom left), courtesy of Kikunoi Honten (bottom right). **Page 122,** photos courtesy of Kinmata (bottom right and left), © Rie Ukai (main). **Page 124,** photos © Noriko Yamaguchi (bottom right), © Kenji Miura (main and bottom left).
Page 126, photos © Yasuo Kubota (bottom left), courtesy of Kodaiji Wakuden (main and bottom right). **Page 128,** photos courtesy of Miyamasou (all). **Page 130,** photos © Satoshi Osaki (bottom left and right), © Suenaga Books, Inc. (main).
Page 132, photos © Satoshi Osaki (all).
Page 134, photos courtesy of Shukahu (all).
Page 136, photos courtesy of Hajime (all).
Page 138, photos © Satoshi Osaki (all).
Page 140, photos courtesy of Kokin Aoyagi (bottom left and right), © Kazuyoshi Miyoshi (main). **Page 144,** photo © William Hereford (main), © Daniel Krieger (bottom left), © Nigel Parry (bottom right).
Page 146, photos © Jose Moran Moya from www.spanishhipster.com (main and bottom right), © Anthony Falco (bottom left).
Page 148, photo © Susie Cushner (bottom left), © Jonathan Young (bottom right), © Antoinette Bruno, StarChefs (main).

Page 150, photos © Nicole Bartelme (main and bottom left), © Michel Ann O'Malley (bottom right). **Page 154,** photos © Evan Sung (main and bottom right), courtesy of Brookyln Fare (bottom left).

Page 156, photos © E. Gilmore (bottom right), © Eric Laignel (bottom left), © T. Schauer (main). **Page 158,** photos © Nicholas Licata (main and bottom right).

Page 160, photos © Jean-Georges Management (bottom right), © Francesco Tonelli (main and bottom left).

Page 162, photos © George Boomer III (all). **Page 164,** photos © Noah Fecks (main), © Melissa Hom (bottom left), © Evan Sung (bottom left). **Page 167,** photo © Jen Munkvold. **Page 168,** photos courtesy of Masa (all). **Page 170,** photos © Noah Kalina (bottom left), © Gabriele Stabile (main and bottom right). **Page 172,** photos courtesy of Per Se (all). **Page 174,** photos © Jose Moran Moya from www.spanishhipster.com (main), © Diane Tapscott (bottom left and right). **Page 176,** photos © Lara Kastner (all).

Page 178, photos © Katherine Bryant (all). **Page 180,** photos © Eric Wolfinger (all). **Page 182,** photo © Gilles Mingasson (bottom right), © Aya Brackett (bottom left), © Eric Wolfinger (main). **Page 184,** photos courtesy of The French Laundry (all).

Page 186, photos courtesy of Shortlist Napa Valley (all). **Page 190,** photos © Pierre Monetta (all). **Page 192,** photos © Ashley Palmer-Watts (main and bottom right), © Neal Haynes (bottom left). **Page 194,** photos courtesy of The Waterside Inn (all).

Page 196, photos © David Griffen Photography, courtesy of www.greatbritishchefs.com (all).

Page 200, photos © Peter Brinch (bottom left), © Thomas Ibsen (bottom right), © Ditte Isager (main). **Page 202,** photos © Götz Wrage (main and bottom right), © Markus Höhn (bottom left).

Page 204, photos © Stefan Liewehr (all). **Page 206,** photos © Mario Reggiani (bottom left and right), © Wowe (main). **Page 208,** photos © Francesca Brambilla/Serena Serrani (main), © Francesco Bolis (bottom left), © Sara Magni (bottom right). **Page 210,** photos © John Brunton (all). **Page 212,** photos © Paolo Terzi (all). **Page 214,** photos © Eneko Diaz (all).

Page 216, photos © David Ruano (bottom right), courtesy of El Celler de Can Roca (bottom left), © Francesc Guillamet (main). **Page 218,** photos © Jose Luis Lopez de Zubiria (main and bottom left), © Oscar Oliva-Puntocolorao (bottom right).

Page 222, photos © Zhangzhang Wuji (main and bottom right), © Head Top Studio (bottom left). **Page 224,** photos © Koo Chi Ho (all). **Page 226,** photos © Koo Chi Ho (all). **Page 228,** photos courtesy of Bukhara (all). **Page 230,** photos courtesy of Indian Accent (all). **Page 232,** photos © Sandesh Ravikumar and The Gateway Hotel & Resorts (all). **Page 234,** photos © John Heng for Iggy's (all). **Page 236,** photos courtesy of Tetsuya's (all).

Page 256, photo of Samir Arora © Dino Baranzelli. **Page 256,** photo of Patricia Wells © Jeff Kauck. **Page 256,** photo of Gael Greene © Diana DeLucia.

Page 257, photo of Ruth Reichl © Marcqui Akins. **Page 258,** photo of Jonathan Gold © Anne Fishbein. **Page 258,** photo of Bruno Verjus © Blast Production. **Page 258,** photo of Alexander Lobrano © Steven Rothfeld. **Page 259,** photo of Charles Campion © Dominick Tyler. **Page 260,** photo of Aun Koh © The Ate Group.

Foodie Top 100 Restaurants Team
Editor & Publisher: Samir Arora
Managing Executive Editor: Erika Lenkert
Book Design: Bonni Evensen
Icon Design: Susan Kare
Map Design: Stuart Silberman
Associate Editor: Allison Johnston
Project Lead: Diane Tapscott

Glam Media's Foodie.com Team
Consumer Products: Sal Arora
Global Creative Director: Victor Zaud
Lifestyle Content Brands: Ryan Stern
Consumer Engineering: Raj Narayan
Consumer Products Producer: Amy Kopp

Foodie.com is Glam Media's social network dedicated to all things food. Tapping in to the knowledge and authority of top chefs, critics, and industry influencers, along with top food authors from the Foodie community, Foodie.com surfaces the best restaurants and recipes for your personalized tastes.

Join the Foodie Top 100 Restaurants conversation at
www.foodie.com/foodie100